YOUR BUSINESS IS A **LEAKY BUCKET**

YOUR BUSINESS
IS A
LEAKY BUCKET

Learn How *to* Avoid Losing Millions
in Revenue *and* Profit Annually

HOWARD M. SHORE

NEW YORK

NASHVILLE • MELBOURNE • VANCOUVER

YOUR BUSINESS IS A LEAKY BUCKET

Learn How *to* Avoid Losing Millions *in* Revenue *and* Profit Annually

Published in New York, New York, by Morgan James Publishing. Morgan James and The Entrepreneurial Publisher are trademarks of Morgan James, LLC.
www.MorganJamesPublishing.com

The Morgan James Speakers Group can bring authors to your live event. For more information or to book an event visit The Morgan James Speakers Group at
www.TheMorganJamesSpeakersGroup.com.

Shelfie

A **free** eBook edition is available
with the purchase of this print book.

CLEARLY PRINT YOUR NAME ABOVE IN UPPER CASE

Instructions to claim your free eBook edition:
1. Download the Shelfie app for Android or iOS
2. Write your name in **UPPER CASE** above
3. Use the Shelfie app to submit a photo
4. Download your eBook to any device

ISBN 978-1-68350-340-8 paperback
ISBN 978-1-68350-341-5 eBook
ISBN 978-1-68350-342-2 hardcover
Library of Congress Control Number:
2016918552

Cover Design by:
Rachel Lopez
www.r2cdesign.com

Interior Design by:
Bonnie Bushman
The Whole Caboodle Graphic Design

In an effort to support local communities, raise awareness and funds, Morgan James Publishing donates a percentage of all book sales for the life of each book to Habitat for Humanity Peninsula and Greater Williamsburg.

Get involved today! Visit
www.MorganJamesBuilds.com

DEDICATION

To Sylvia, thank you for choosing to share your life with
me. You have always inspired me to become a better
husband, father, son, family member, and human being.

To Michael and Gabriel, may you always act with
character that will lead to continuous happiness.

TABLE OF CONTENTS

ACKNOWLEDGMENTS

Thank You!

I want to thank the many CEOs and executives who have given me the honor of being part of their success journeys. As I have always said, we gain wisdom together! It is through our experiences together that I was able to accumulate the knowledge, experience, and insight that I now share in this book. Through our obstacles and challenges I have been able to distill a wealth of information I could not wait to share with you.

Key Contributors:

Several people went above and beyond the call of duty to help turn me into an author. I must start with two wonderful, intelligent, and remarkable women who I am blessed to have in my life: my wife Sylvia Medina-Shore and mom Sheryl Shore. They are great inspirations to me in their different ways and were crucial in the final editing and shaping of the book.

Other key contributors who helped shape my book are: Jerry Fons (President, Executive Power); Umesh Jain (CEO, Now Analytics); Jeff Redmon (Principal, Redmon Law and Justin Spizman (Justin Spizman Book Architect)

Gazelles

Gazelles, Inc. and Gazelles International deserve a special thank you. My partnership with the Gazelles organizations has been nothing short of a remarkable journey. Their imprint on what I know and continue to learn has been an inflection point for me and my clients. The depth of the intellectual capital they provide to the coaches, the ongoing learning at the Scaling Up summits, and the continuous learning keep me sharp.

I would be remiss if I did not recognize my mastermind group. This is the handpicked group of senior Gazelles Coaches that meet with me once each month: David Chavez, Elizabeth Crook, Jerry Fons, Ron Huntington, Jon Iveson, Jim Jubelirer, Cleo Maheux, Jeff Redmon. They are outstanding coaches, ladies and gentlemen. Each month we continue to challenge each other to raise the bar on how to become better coaches, business people, family members, and citizens. While I consider all Gazelles Coaches to be extraordinary, this is definitely an elite unit.

Thought Leaders

I am so thankful for the many thought leaders that have helped influence and shape my ideas. Just like running a company, it takes the knowledge and experience of many to get the best results.

Harry Spanos was my direct supervisor and mentor when we were employed at Ryder. Many years ago, Harry introduced the "leaky bucket" concept in our strategic planning process.

While I cite some of their works at the end of this book, I want to recognize a few of the key gurus that who have really influenced this book: Jim Collins, Stephen Covey, Verne Harnish, Patrick Lencioni, Jim Loehr, W. Chan Kim, Renée Mauborgne, Alexander Osterwalder, Tom Peters, Yves Pigneur, and Bradford D. Smart.

FOREWORD

Howard Shore and I met more than eight years ago when he became affiliated with my executive education organization, Gazelles, Inc. as a coach. It quickly became clear that he has a remarkable impact on every entrepreneur he meets, listening attentively before firmly addressing the hard issues in their businesses.

Getting results is rooted in Howard's DNA. He became one of our first Certified Coaches and has helped many clients implement the Scaling Up tools successfully. From the beginning, Howard has been a leader in the Gazelles International organization, mentoring others, contributing to our intellectual capital, assisting in the development of my book *Scaling Up*, and developing our community of coaches by conducting workshops at our Coaches Summits. Our organization recognized him with our "Practice What You Preach." core values award. All who know him find that he believes strongly in being respectful, acting with integrity, being consistent, and constantly pursuing mastery. Beyond being an outstanding colleague, he has become a trusted friend.

In this practical guide, Howard inspires company leaders to make purposeful changes that will ignite growth and lead their organizations to greatness. He addresses the 15 most common challenges in the areas of strategy, execution, and people, carefully describing each of the issues, providing stories of real client situations, and suggesting solutions you can apply immediately. Understanding and addressing these issues appropriately will lead to unprecedented growth and profitability, while reducing the stress and drama that are characteristics of undisciplined operations.

One of the most interesting topics Howard addresses is the "Leaky Bucket Principle," in which the bigger and more complex the business, the leakier the bucket. Every leader will benefit from his analysis of our mindsets and the unintentional influence they have on our organizations' leaks. The first leak is often poor leadership, and Howard provides practical insight on how to grow as a leader and fix the problem. He also provides on-the-ground insights into how to use improve on strategy and execution, two other pillars of the Scaling Up system. If you are looking to learn more about the Scaling Up system, elevate your business and get measurable results, this book is a must-read.

Verne Harnish
CEO, Gazelles
Author of *Scaling Up (Rockefeller Habits 2.0)*, *The Greatest Business Decisions of All Time*, and *Mastering the Rockefeller Habits*

PART I

IS YOUR BUCKET LEAKING?

"The most dangerous kind of waste is the waste we do not recognize."
—Shigeo Shingo[1]

Chapter 1

THE LEAKY BUCKET
PRINCIPLE

magine you have built a plan; your leadership team is functioning at an extremely high level; you have created a strong culture of accountability; and the entire organization is running on all cylinders! That is what happened for one company in the insurance brokerage industry that mastered application of the Leaky Bucket Principle.

This company was doing extremely well and had an aggressive growth plan for the year. The executive team realized that the biggest bottleneck for their organization was finding good talent. They believed their ability to add talent could not keep pace with their growth plan. They decided to attack their problem from a different vantage point. What if there was less work to be done? Or if they could get their existing workforce to handle more work and not have to work more hours?

During their two-day planning session with me, their coach, they focused on the idea of reducing 35,000 hours of work without eliminating any employees. The discussion concluded on the idea of shifting their organizational lens to "eliminating waste" as they believed they were operating very inefficiently. Many of their processes were antiquated, departments were working at cross-purposes, and many things people were doing added little to no value to getting, keeping, or growing customer relationships. The leadership team believed, and ultimately proved correct, that, on average, all employees could eliminate at least 10 percent waste, or four hours per week of unnecessary workload.

Without going into detail, the organization rallied every employee to develop legitimate ideas on eliminating unnecessary activities and identifying practices that could result in reducing hours worked. By the end of 90 days they had identified more than 40,000 hours of real work that could be eliminated. By the end of six months, they exceeded even their most optimistic levels of new customer acquisition, implemented many of the hour-reduction initiatives, and employee satisfaction was the highest it had ever been. They will tell you this never would have happened had they not applied the concepts in this book!

Being Successful in Business Has Not Changed

Today's storyline may be different, but success in business has not changed—only the times, the tools you might use, and the playing field have been altered. To succeed in business, leaders must have a business operating system that allows their team members to make clear decisions and take action regardless of the noise. Success is the result of how well your business operating system is functioning. Throughout the last hundred years and into the next hundred, you will find all of your challenges are the consequence of how effective you are in three areas:

1. People
2. Strategy
3. Execution

The People. As Jim Collins stated in his book *Good to Great*, "first who then what."[2] Too often businesses get stuck because their employees can't help them grow to the next level. Are the people commanding your ship acting like a lid, containing its growth? If you have people problems in the middle or at the bottom of the ship, know that the nexus of the issue resides at the top. If you have the right people at the helm of the ship, the rest of your personnel decisions will follow accordingly. Everything starts at the top and rolls downhill.

The people, culture, structure, and policies related to them have to evolve with the organization, and sometimes the organization outgrows them. Understand that the right people are only those people who live all of your core values. Your organizational structure must support its strategy, and the right people should be in the right roles and asked to do the right things. Leaders must be fanatical about having the very best recruiting and onboarding processes and must be willing to move on from the wrong people quickly.

The Strategy. Strategy has two dimensions: internal and external. The external dimension addresses growth. There is more supply than there is demand in all industries. You cannot approach business without considering the many others who want to attract the same customer you do. As a result, carefully consider why and how a customer will choose you over everyone else. Have a soundly constructed approach to acquire them. The external dimension is insufficient if you are not growing faster than the market.

The second dimension is your internal strategy. This is about creating a business model that will turn your revenue into a sizeable profit and produce sufficient cash. If you generate revenue that cannot produce adequate cash, you will go bankrupt! You know you have a bad business model if you do not have an abundance of cash.

The Execution. Your priorities are clear, everyone is aligned to the same priorities, and accountability is strong. Execution is strong when you consistently achieve annual and quarterly priorities. This is about using the right metrics and data to properly motivate everyone on a daily basis. Each employee understands whether it was a good or bad day. Your indicators sufficiently lead the team to make the decisions that need to be made.

You have a problem with execution when the organization is more reactive than proactive. Communication in your organization may be insufficient, leading to confusion, mistakes, finger-pointing, and frustration. More importantly, your team is not hitting monthly revenue and profit goals.

The Leaky Bucket

Most companies have a lot more growth and profit potential staring them right in the face. Having a great team is right around the corner, but they can't see it. Less stress, more control over the business, less drama, and happy customers can be more simply attained. The secret can be found in their "Leaky Bucket." In the early years your bucket is small and manageable, given that you only have a few customers and employees. Even if leaks are everywhere, it is a small bucket. Dealing with leaks is a nuisance but does not seem daunting. However, as you grow, so does your bucket. The more layers of management, processes, complexity, customers, employees, systems, etc. pouring into the bucket, the more that can leak out. All of a sudden what did not seem like a big problem becomes serious.

The Leaky Bucket concept is very important. The leaks this book will cover will not be found in your financial statements. Yes, they impact the results but not in ways that are easily measured. As you read and think about leaks from here on out, you need to visualize cash pouring out of a bucket through lots of various sized holes. You can also imagine water flowing over the top because the bucket has not grown fast enough.

This is the Leaky Bucket Principle, and all companies have Leaky Buckets. That is not to say your accountants are wrong. The concept of generally accepted accounting principles is sound and needed. However, here's where accounting fails us: Your financial statements can be correct, yet you could still go out of business. No financial statement will show all the places where a business is failing. In other words, where would one go to examine and understand one's Leaky Bucket? When addressing leaks, the numbers often are much bigger than the numbers the financial statements are capturing. It's frustrating when your employees are already doing the work and cash is leaking right before your and their eyes.

Here are examples of the cash leaks I am talking about:

- Weak salespeople who cannot close or get to the decision maker
- Lack of strategy
- Keeping the wrong employees

- Accountability failure
- Poor communication
- Unfilled positions or underinvestment in functions
- Poor prioritization and alignment
- Trying to serve too many customer segments at one time
- Lack of differentiation
- Broken processes
- High employee turnover
- Demotivating your employees
- Lack of leadership

Regardless of how you choose to fill your proverbial bucket, aim to fill it to the brim and keep increasing the size of your bucket. The tools, concepts, and processes addressed in this book are practical and are presented in simple terms. You may have heard of some or all of them and, if honest, are not giving them the attention they deserve. Leaders are not quantifying how big these leaks are because they are not easily quantified and they are issues leaders prefer not to address. Identifying the leaks forces leaders to stop and work *on* the business rather than *in* it. Most leaders when honest have a preference for action—even if they know those actions are not working.

As you consider whether to read this book, each chapter offers a different way to close cash leaks—cash that is already available to you. The bigger your business, the greater your leaks. Be a heat-seeking missile for money. Prioritize the more meaningful and greater leaks first!

You will find this book worth reading if you would like to have a lot more profit and cash, and if you believe the answer should be "yes" to the following questions:

- Does every person in your organization live the same core values?
- Do you set lofty standards for outcomes for every role in your company, and has every employee met them?
- Do you raise those standards every year?
- Have you reduced your cost and time for acquiring new customers?

- Have you increased your customer retention rate?
- Have you closed a higher percentage of your opportunities?
- Have fewer mistakes occurred?
- Do you have the highest performing team in the industry?
- Has product quality risen?
- Have you increased the gross margin you generated for every dollar you spent in salary?

As a leader or business owner, you have four important responsibilities:

1. *Create a system and evaluation process to identify your largest leaks.*
2. *Develop action plans to close the leaks when they occur.*
3. *Establish accountability protocols to make sure the action plans effectively occur.*
4. *Repeat steps 1, 2, and 3.*

I met with a company that did over $200 million in quotes the previous year, but only generated $16 million in revenue. The good news: They had captured the full value of the business they had quoted during the year, which is not required by generally accepted accounting principles. The bad news: They had come to accept that they would lose a large number of their bids. When I asked how many of these bids were lost because of pricing mistakes, broken relationships, and other issues that could be addressed by the company, they couldn't provide an answer.

So, what is the point of this example? Leaks are everywhere. They hide in every crevice, corner, and undetectable hole within your business. They can be slow bleeds or so substantial they break the bucket in two. Regardless of how the leaks appear, the Leaky Bucket Principle stands for the idea that your bucket leaks cut into your profits, purpose, or overall mission, whatever that may look like, and can eventually become so unmanageable that they can end your business.

Once you've acknowledged that leaks are part of normal business operations, you can then understand where the leaks are most likely to appear and address these areas quickly—and with decisive and curative measures. Colin Powell said,

"There are no secrets to success. It is the result of preparation, hard work, and learning from failure."[3] Bucket leaks are not necessarily failure, but failing to address them will absolutely lead to it.

So with that said, the remainder of this book will work to help you build the necessary game plan to locate leaks and eliminate them.

Chapter 2

IS YOUR BUSINESS
A LEAKY BUCKET?

T hat is truly the million-dollar question. We will not only determine how your business *is* a Leaky Bucket, we will also provide you with actionable ideas on how to plug those holes when they develop. Albert Einstein said, "If I had an hour to solve a problem I'd spend fifty-five minutes thinking about the problem and five minutes thinking about solutions."[4] It takes thought followed by proper planning to evaluate your bucket before you can begin resolving the issues at hand. So now, let's begin to determine how your business is a Leaky Bucket.

It's a difficult time to be a leader in today's business environment. The rate of change, volume of available information, and employee challenges can make your role exciting, frustrating, and overwhelming all in the same day. Leaders are often faced head-on, eye-to-eye with questions like:

Do you feel unprepared to deal with today's business challenges?
Do some key problems recur month after month and year after year?
Are you having difficulty building the team you can trust to get things done?

Does it seem like people are not working together toward common goals and priorities?

Do you wish you had a better system for holding people accountable?

If you answered yes to some or all of these questions, you are part of the norm. From my perspective, three concerns could be at play if you didn't answer yes to most (if not all) of these questions:

1. You are in denial or naïve and do not recognize the issues exist.
2. You recognize the issues and either don't believe they are serious enough to deal with or don't believe you can improve them.
3. You do not like dealing with soft-skills issues and just avoid them altogether.

If you fall into any of these categories, ultimately you will experience more stress, less revenue, and lower profit margins than you should. Admitting that you have a problem is the first step toward fixing it.

Most leaders, especially entrepreneurs, deal with this challenge: They are leading and managing their businesses with broken or nonexistent processes. Consequently, they improperly identify, discuss, and address opportunities for growth, profit, and productivity.

One challenge I have with every leader I meet, regardless of their level of success, is how to respectfully help them understand that they have revenue and profit leaks everywhere and that these leaks are much larger than they realize. The bigger challenge is helping them appreciate that they could be doing a lot more to address those leaks. Not addressing some of your leaks can lead to severe and possibly fatal consequences for the business.

Rarely will you find a product or service that is truly unique in today's business environment. Even when a company develops a way to deliver its product or service that differentiates it from the competition, most of the time there is no legal means to prevent others from promptly copying the method, so the advantage goes away quickly. Two elements that certainly differentiate your business from your competition are:

1. Your people and
2. Your company's culture.

Not surprisingly, those are the two areas where most leaks occur. If you develop and maintain a strong group of team members and a high-quality culture, you will create an ironclad bucket. But if neither or just one is strong, you are a prime candidate for plenty of holes. Because so many leaders give this topic lip service but do little to master the task of building an outstanding team from top to bottom, let's start by talking about the people.

Ten Signs of a "Sleepy" Team

A sleepy team is just what it sounds like: an organization that suffers greatly because its drivers are literally asleep at the wheel, not maintaining focus to evaluate what not only is directly in front of them but also what lurks in the blind spots around the car. Many signs of a sleepy team exist, and there is a direct and causal relationship with businesses that are sleepy and leaky; they are intimately connected to one another.

Most leaders say they want to hire top people. They say they will not accept mediocrity on their teams. They say they have pride in the people who work for them. But this is not always the case. As you begin to peel back the layers of any organization, it becomes quite clear that some leaders do not practice what they preach.

It is easy to say, "I want to hire a great team." However, this is usually difficult to accomplish. As previously mentioned, leaks occur everywhere. And when it comes to your people, the easiest way to tell whether they are part of the reasons your bucket is leaking is to consider the statements below. Take time to put a checkmark next to each one of the circumstances below that exist in your business:

❑ We continue to struggle to acquire new customers.
❑ Our growth rate percentage has not exceeded industry averages in each of the last three years.

❏ Our net profit margin percentage is not consistent or is nothing to be proud of. In other words, we are at industry average or below.

❏ Only a few employees in our organization give that extra effort, and we have trouble motivating the rest.

❏ Positions are created or altered to fit an existing employee instead of finding the right employee to fit a position.

❏ Management tolerates consistent and repeated mistakes by an individual.

❏ People wait around to be told what to do rather than figuring it out themselves.

❏ There is little innovation in each position.

❏ You find higher overall turnover than your direct competitors in key positions.

❏ Management spends more time "doing" instead of coaching, mentoring, recruiting, and holding people accountable.

This is an extensive but not a complete checklist. Obviously many more shortcomings could impact your business, but this list is a great place to start identifying and prioritizing the leaks in your bucket. A checkmark may or may not indicate a serious problem but does represent a leak in your bucket. These problems result in lost revenue, increased costs, and lower margins. Many times leaders are under the misconception that they do not have a choice, that the status quo is the only way they can do business. Ironically, they find it more comfortable not to deal with the issues and consequences I've described than to learn how to build the appropriate organizational structure, better define positions, and be smarter about hiring. By taking the time up front to do it right, they would grow faster, have more time, reduce costs, and expand margins. Instead, they choose to do what is comfortable.

Ten Signs of a "Sleepy" Culture

Remember, it is not just about the people. Leaks in your business are often caused by the culture in which your team resides. The company's environment is as important as the people themselves. Specifically, let's take a few minutes to determine whether your company maintains a strong culture. Check each box that applies to you. The more boxes you check, the better off you are.

- ❏ We have a regular system for measuring and monitoring employee adherence to core values.
- ❏ We have always fired employees who failed to consistently meet core values daily in response to performance improvement plans.
- ❏ All executives and middle managers refer back to core values when giving praise or reprimands.
- ❏ We encourage all employees to engage in constructive debate over issues.
- ❏ Many of our decisions are made by front-line employees.
- ❏ Every employee believes someone is genuinely interested and actively participates in their development.
- ❏ Our communication and meetings systems function so well that information moves through the organization rapidly and quickly.
- ❏ We have an effective process for collecting regular employee input and putting that information into action.
- ❏ Customer feedback and data is comprehensive, frequent, and accurate, and we use this information to improve our business.
- ❏ We have established key performance indicators for all positions in such a way that every employee knows whether they had a good day and week.

Gallup Survey questions provide another way to look at this. These include the following checkpoints that allow you to assess the strength of the culture found within your organization. The survey has every employee rate how strongly they agree with each one of the following statements, using a scale from one to ten. One signifies that they **strongly disagree** with the statement, and 10 signifies that they **strongly agree** with the statement:

- I know what is expected of me at work.
- I have the materials and equipment I need to do my work properly.
- At work, I have the opportunity to do what I do best every day.

- In the last seven days, I have received recognition or praise for doing good work.
- My supervisor, or someone at work, seems to care about me as a person.
- There is someone at work who encourages my development.
- At work, my opinions seem to count.
- The mission or purpose of my company makes me feel my job is important.
- My associates or fellow employees are committed to doing quality work.
- I have a best friend at work.
- In the last six months, someone at work has talked to me about my progress.
- This last year, I have had opportunities to learn and grow.[5]

Moving forward, when we ask whether your business is a Leaky Bucket, your answer ought to be: "Of course it is!" The other point is that finding and closing leaks is a never-ending journey for the leadership team. That was this chapter's goal: To demonstrate that your business suffers from the same problems that all other businesses face.

If you are like most leaders, you probably completed the above surveys, found thinking about addressing so many issues exhausting, and wondered if you are up for the challenge. As many other leaders before have found, the correct answer is a resounding yes! Humble leaders learn that we spend the rest of our lives learning to master the techniques of running a business. Your job is to continually identify metrics that tell you how each process and role is functioning and then challenge everyone to set new company performance goals. The rest of this book will focus on helping you learn how to address the most common business leaks and ensuring your bucket is lined with the strongest materials.

—— $\dashv$ *Chapter 3* $\vdash$ ——

LEADERSHIP MINDSETS
CAUSING LEAKS

This book is all about finding and fixing the weaknesses damaging your business. From my perspective, there is no better place to start than by taking a look at the top of your company to determine where these slow and even fast leaks are occurring. Leadership is essential to the success of any business, big or small. Show me a great leader, and I bet a strong business is following close behind.

If you are in a leadership position, it is crucial to have a basic understanding of the type of leader you are. Your mindset and the corresponding actions will often dictate just how organized and successful your business can be. So we will start our head-to-toe evaluation of your business with the man or woman up front.

Are you worried that while your business may appear to be a full bucket, it is actually slowly emptying under your watchful eye? If so, you are not alone. This is a concern for all business owners. If your bucket is leaking, you can absolutely assume your business is losing potential profit and may be quickly losing its competitive advantage. This is a scary proposition, but one we all have to get really comfortable with. The more holes in your bucket, the higher the likelihood that your business will eventually come to a screeching halt or capsize completely.

Fundamentally speaking, buckets leak for many reasons, and we will cover them in the remainder of the book. Before we get to them, however, we have to do a little self-reflection. After all, who cares about a Leaky Bucket when there is nothing in it to begin with?

What Type of CEO Are You?

An important question you need to ask is "What kind of CEO/leader am I?" The next question you must ponder is "How balanced is my strategic decision-making?" Why do you need to ask these questions? Because I have seen organizations drive their strategy through three lenses:

- Growth Orientation
- Product/Service Orientation
- Waste Orientation

A business model is only effective if it addresses all three lenses. Nevertheless, the majority of business leaders only address one or two. Usually they are either very product/service-oriented or growth-oriented, but not both. Being over-weighted in one lens leads to tremendous waste and leaks without them realizing it. Rather than fixing the fact that they are over-weighted in one area, they will start cutting costs in their weakest area. For example, if you are a product- or service-oriented leader, your sales and marketing function is probably not producing sufficiently. In these cases, it is common to find underinvestment in that function, and in some cases leaders cut costs while continuing to invest heavily in improving products and services because that is their strength. This move is justified by the fact that the customers you do have love you! The problem, however, is that the extra love does not result in enough growth, and in many cases the extra cost of delivering added service and product features results in waste. It is waste because the market will not accept the pricing needed to justify all the added features and benefits. Customers will be happy to take what you are offering for free but are not willing to pay for it.

Are You a Growth-Oriented Leader?

Growth-oriented leaders focus most of their organization's energy on sales and marketing activities. It is common to hear in these organizations that "More sales will make all your problems go away." The CEO may have grown up in sales, and in many businesses that is what you do. In some cases, there is a heavy emphasis on getting volume up and worrying about making money sometime in the future. This has been very common in the new cyber-platform world. Getting users and giving free services is the soup du jour, the thought being that he who owns the most users wins.

In insurance brokerages and similar industries, the primary business is to sell and service customers. It is natural to have this focus. However, while it may be good that you are a natural heat-seeking missile for customers, you also need to recognize and remove waste in your organization and build a successful service model. Many growth-oriented CEOs are prone to quick growth and either go bankrupt or need to give up too much of their equity to others to feed their revenue habit. If you are consistently growing 25 percent or more per quarter and have a sizeable business, you probably do not need to spend time in the strategy chapters and need to move quickly to the execution and people sections.

Are You a Product- or Service-Oriented Leader?

The product- or service-oriented leaders are masters of their craft, always focused on perfecting their product and service. Usually, they are excellent at what they do. They can demonstrate tons of metrics proving why they are better than everyone else, but they do not have the revenue to show for it. They spend all their time perfecting processes and creating the perfect products and services. In these organizations we have to watch for three common problems: 1) they undercharge for their products and services relative to what they cost; 2) they give away features and benefits they can charge for; and 3) they focus on things that are not important to their customer. They feel their actions are justified because they commonly get customers that stay with them forever.

The perennial problem for this type of leader is getting more customers. They have a tendency to grow much slower than is necessary. Their mantra is to grow smartly, and they are always concerned whether they can service and support that growth. Unfortunately, this tendency almost always hampers your true growth potential. You must round out your leadership team with people who will really challenge your thinking around sales and marketing.

Are You a Waste-Oriented Leader?

The waste-oriented leader has key performance indicators, goals, and targets for everything. They look at the sales and product/service lenses and determine how both lenses are operating as they relate to their purpose and the needs of the core customer(s). They are constantly asking the questions:

- How efficient are we at making our products and delivering our services?
- Are we achieving high standards of quality for our products and services in the critical needs of our core customers and then making the tough decisions in areas that are not important to our customers so we can reduce our costs?
- Are costs optimized to acquire each new customer?
- Are we doing the right things to preserve our relationships with existing customers to minimize lost customers and to get them to spend more with us?
- Are we elevating our employee relationships to increase our employee engagement and retention and to attract top talent?

Conflict Between Sales and Operations Is Necessary

A never-ending conflict between sales and operations is the real challenge. They often bang up against one another, so if you do not find a lot of conflict between the two in your organization, then you know you have a problem. Your leaks will be larger than organizations that have more balance in their leadership thinking. Growth without discipline and making choices creates a lot of waste and burns cash.

This leadership issue is critical because many CEOs are not mindful of the need for balance when building their leadership teams. Likely they are sales oriented or product/service oriented. Generally, they prefer to hire people who they feel think like them. Consider this when you read the people section and ask questions like: Do you have enough of the right types of people on your team to scale the company? Do you have a tendency to squeeze out the opposite type of person because of your preference?

Two Important Questions for Every Business Owner

1. *Are you ignoring a bad business strategy?*
2. *Are you playing to win OR not to lose?*

These questions are important rabbit holes to dive into. They may seem frightening at first, because the answers could shed light on some serious problems within your business. However, if you're ignoring bad business practices, or playing so conservatively that you'll never grow, you won't have to worry about your bucket leaking—likely you'll never fill it in the first place.

Now, let's look at two very important questions.

Are You Ignoring a Bad Business Strategy?

"However beautiful the strategy, you should occasionally look at the results," a sentence often incorrectly attributed to Winston Churchill, is where we will begin.[6] Survey not only where you stand, but also look back over your shoulder and think about how you got there. Every business in creation should have a well-considered and planned-out business strategy. If you haven't thought of one or created one, you have some work to do. However, if you have at least a basic business strategy, you need to determine whether it has growth and scaling potential.

Your business strategy is a determining factor in whether your sales will or will not grow faster than your competition's. Sounds enticing, right? While many factors weigh into whether you have a strong business strategy, I like to start with asking this question:

Does your business have an "unusual offering" that is critical in the buying decision of your target customer?

Most businesses have an unusual offering their prospects don't know about, or they don't have one and are not facing it. If you have a specific offering, then analyze how you present your product or service to the public. Do you do so in a way that works to monetize it? Do you put your best foot forward, inviting consumers in through a well-crafted sales pitch? It all makes a substantial difference.

An unusual offering is most commonly referred to as a "unique value proposition" or how you differentiate your product and services from those offered by your competition. I've chosen the word "unusual" instead of "unique" for a reason. While the difference between the two words is subtle, the standard for "unusual" is much more achievable for most businesses. Unique offerings are very difficult to create and almost impossible to sustain for very long.

The best businesses have mastered consistency in unusual offerings. For example, everyone in the fast food industry knows they are supposed to deliver consistent quality in food, fast, and yet they don't. McDonald's has a better track record in terms of quickly moving customers through lines than other fast food restaurants. Likewise, when it comes to customer service, Nordstrom has been able to set themselves apart from competitors who claim high-quality service as their differentiator.

Your unusual offering needs to change over time with the market. For example, FedEx used to focus its business differentiator on "when it absolutely, positively has to be there overnight." This is no longer a business differentiator because all of the competition caught up, and now customers expect that level of service. Even the United States Postal Service can consistently deliver on that promise. So FedEx adjusted by not just delivering the package on time, but by doing so in a professional, customer-centric, and reliable manner. The concept seems to be the same, but the adjustment in the business strategy is crucial to their success.

Your ability to grow sales rests on:

1. How well do you understand your core customer? Who are they as people? What problems do they need solved? How do they expect to be treated? What are their circumstances?

2. How well do you match your products and services to their needs and help them see that you understand them and are best positioned to serve them?

3. Does your internal strategy focus on being best in the world at delivering those products and services and in a way that your customer can recognize you are different? Can you be their champion?

Great salespeople cannot erase a bad strategy, no matter how often people say they can. This is an important point to understand because so many people want to try to "fight fire with fire." They believe if the house is burning, you just need to send in better firefighters. The truth is that you need more water and a better plan to distribute that water across the flames. The same is true in business. You can't just fight the fires in your business by hiring a better team to fight them. The better practice: Implement a more thoughtful and well-considered strategy that eliminates the causes for fires and the need for firefighters. In fact, if you have a great strategy you can actually compensate for a lot of other holes, including a weak sales force.

Maintaining a strong strategy involves evaluating how to grow your sales in the right way. When sales are not growing, it is usually the result of a bad business strategy. Most companies fail to recognize and address inadequate sales growth as a strategy issue.[7] First, sales management and the salespeople are blamed. This can go on for years. Salespeople come and go with no change in result! Next, someone will decide it is a marketing problem. You'll hear statements like, "We just need to do a better job of getting our name out there, learn to better leverage the internet to get leads, and everything will turn around."

When that fails, the economy becomes the culprit. There is too much competition, consumers aren't spending money, and times have changed. In most situations, leaders are the real root of the problem—they have ignored the fact that their sales offering is inadequate and that the marketplace has spoken.

In crisis, everyone becomes a finger-pointer. But if you create and implement a strong business strategy, fewer crises will occur and fewer people will point their fingers in unwarranted directions when they do.

Constant turnover in your sales force and constant leadership complaints about failing salespeople indicate that your business is operating under a bad strategy. A bad business strategy results in sending good salespeople out to get slaughtered. In my experience, when you have a good strategy, even a bad salesperson can sell your product or service. In fact, you will find that companies with great strategies often only need people willing to take incoming orders and don't really have salespeople.

When you have a good strategy, salespeople line up at your door to work for you. Too often leaders are hoping and praying that hiring great salespeople will magically make a bad strategy disappear. So the real question is:

What unusual offering can your sales force promote to attract the customer segment you've defined as your prime target?

Answer that question, and you will likely position yourself to create a fantastic business. And once you create a thoughtful strategy, then you can begin to fill your bucket, but only if you combine a winning business strategy with a winning desire and attitude.

Are You Playing to Win or Not to Lose?

Emotions were running high in the last quarter of 2008, with the banking debacle, stock market meltdown, the soaring foreclosure rate, job losses, poor earnings reports, and dismal projections. Finally, the government, which had long denied the obvious, admitted that we were experiencing an economic recession.

Nobody wanted to use the word "depression" about the economy, but that's the word that best described the country's mood. The result: Businesses and consumers put on the brakes. Most everyone started operating in a "playing not to lose" mindset. They stopped trying to win and completely went on the defensive. However, for a small group of Americans, opportunity had just knocked. They took advantage of the inexpensive real estate market, stole market share, acquired quality talent, and bought stocks and other investment products at bargain-basement prices. In the process, they ended up making millions of dollars.

Great leaders and strong businesses recognize opportunities to fill buckets and proceed accordingly. Their desire to win is so strong it overcomes their fear of losing. They do it through sheer will and the right balance of a positive attitude. I am hopeful your business does not find itself in the dire situation we experienced in 2008, but the absence of dire circumstances doesn't mean attitude and desire shouldn't remain similar to that of the small group of Americans who were opportunistic and took advantage of the situation. A "scared to lose" mentality can be costly for your career or your business.

The mind does funny things when negative events occur. We have to look no further than what has transpired in our government over the last several years. Leonard Pitts's article in the *Miami Herald* titled "Mindless Zeal Not Conducive to Thoughtful Reasoning" really captures the essence of what has gone wrong in people's thought processes. He writes about a reader whose letter to the editor attacked him for writing negative articles on President George W. Bush during his second term. Without rehashing the article, Pitts argues that the real issue is what happens when people are so loyal to their own ideology that they lose sight of the bigger picture. He points to Rush Limbaugh's comment, "I hope he [Obama] fails," as a prime example of this. The reality is that if Obama failed, it would impact us all in extremely detrimental ways.[8]

Five Common Bad Decisions Drawn from Weakness

Negative events result when people fail to look at their businesses and careers in the right way. When you aim to preserve the status quo, it is not unusual to draw some conclusions like these:

- Decide *not* to replace "B" and "C" players with "A" players, using cost as an excuse. This is a silly decision because "A" players can do the work of as many as three average players. "A" players are employees who consistently meet productivity requirements (performance standards) and consistently live your company's core values.[9] If you hire "A" players, your overall wage costs will actually be lower as a percentage of revenue because fewer people accomplish better results.[10]

- Stop advertising. This decision, in some circumstances, results in a threefold increase in the acquisition cost per customer in the long run and dramatically reduces the leads that come to the sales force. In other words, you increase your costs and reduce your sales.

- Fail to do the things that create a positive environment for your salespeople and cut off training. Employees thrive on positive energy; when they lack it, they do not take on extra assignments, do not develop innovative ideas, and are not at the top of their game. In the end your business suffers.

- Management accepts a sluggish economy as an excuse for not meeting targets and stops holding people accountable. *Common logic leads us to conclude that most companies own less than 1 percent market share within their target market. Therefore, there is no reason not to grow and achieve targets. All that is needed is execution of a good strategy.*

- Executives become very conservative and averse to any risk in their decisions. This usually means doing what they have always done. Following that logic, if you had a bad year last year, you know what you can expect this year. In addition, you miss challenging your people to see the opportunities that are right in front of them.

These practices can be so harmful because, fundamentally, they do nothing to fill your bucket. While an empty bucket does not leak, if you are not playing to win, you are only playing not to lose—which will eventually cause you to lose. It may not be today, or tomorrow, or even a month from now. But like those that came before, you will eventually hit the skids and lose.

I challenge you to determine how you are allowing negative people and your environment to prevent you from filling your bucket to the brim. If everyone was playing to win within your value system every minute of every day, what would or could they be doing differently? What are the top one or two things you could be doing right now to make a difference for your company? Are you spending the majority of your time focusing on that? If not, can you really say you are playing to win? Michael Jordan said, "I play to win, whether during practice or a real game. And I will not let anything get in the way of me and my competitive enthusiasm to win."[11] The same could be true for you and your business. You have to play to win. Its value is almost immeasurable. Creating a strong business plan and strategy will help you play to win. Maintaining an opportunistic attitude and even remaining open to assessing and taking risk will help you win.

Attitude is a critical component of success, and you have to maintain an attitude consistent with filling your bucket. Leaks empty your bucket, but you won't have to worry about leaks if you never put anything into your bucket in the first place. As you'll quickly find out, it is much easier to fill the bucket than to maintain it. You surely will have to learn how to walk before you run. As we move through this book, keep in the back of your mind the importance of maintaining fantastic business strategy and a winning attitude. You'll need them both to make it to your destination.

$\vdash$ *Chapter 4* $\dashv$

MODERN-DAY
PROFIT LEAKS

I n the previous chapter, we placed a mirror in front of your company to
determine if you had the culture or the people in place that could conceivably
cause leaks in your business. Now we'll take this analysis one step further and
discuss what actual modern-day profit leaks could look like for your business and
how to evaluate them.

As stated in Chapter 1, most modern-day profit leaks occur in three distinct
areas of your business:

1. Your people
2. Your strategy
3. Your execution

Certainly, leaks can occur anywhere, but I have found that the vast majority
of leaks fall under these three categories. Now, let's take a look at the list of profit
leaks likely plaguing your company. These include:

People Leaks

People leaks cause unnecessary problems within your organization. These unproductive dramas take leaders' and mid-managers' time and attention away from being strategic, interfacing with customers and other key stakeholders, and having more productive interactions with their team.

Profit Leak #1: *Poor Leadership*

When you make allowances for poor leadership, you are deciding that a substandard leader has more to offer than everyone else put together, which is a fool's bet. Your ineffective leader causes everyone else to perform at lower levels. You lose access to a lot of great ideas, and people are less apt to willingly give extra effort.

Profit Leak #2: *"B" and "C" Players*

This leak occurs when your internal processes do not properly identify "B" and "C" performers and take too long to take action even after you identify them. Additionally, you may be classifying people as "A" players for the wrong reasons, while the real "A" players quit, get fired, or become less engaged in their positions.

Profit Leak #3: *Financial Transparency*

"Revenue is vanity, profit is sanity, and cash is king."[12] How well do you understand what drives your cash position? Does your entire team understand how their actions affect cash? Can they see this impact? Have you established expectations as to how each member of the team is going to improve cash?

Profit Leak #4: *Vacant Positions*

Many of your challenges may result from how much emphasis you place on having strategies to limit the amount of time that positions remain vacant. They may also occur because of failure to create positions that need to exist. Filling open positions with the wrong level of talent because of the compensation level you have set for the position is another pitfall. Most organizations are so caught up on what a position will cost them that they lose big opportunities to hire people who can bring in revenue and operational efficiency that far exceeds their earnings package. Existing people get burned out trying to make up for the missing employee, and current efforts are not executed well because people are spread too thin.

Profit Leak #5: *Excessive Turnover*

How much does it cost you to find each new person? How long does it take you to build a new employee's institutional knowledge? What impact does that have on customers? What impact does it have on the overall flow of the organization? How does it affect productivity? How much time does it take to train a new hire? How does it affect the trainer's productivity? When you add it all up, what does turnover cost your company each year?

Strategy Leaks

We analyze strategy leaks in two ways. On the one hand, we consider whether your company is growing at an acceptably high level, whether this growth rate is predictable, and whether you believe it will continue for the next several years. On the other hand, does your business model create sufficient cash flow? Again, revenue is vanity, profit is sanity, and cash is king!

Profit Leak #6: *Action Without Purpose*

The day you start your business, you had better place "purpose" at its forefront. This is a critical issue that fails to get enough attention. Many business owners who are asked, "What is the purpose of your business?" will answer "to make money" (or something similar). You may be thinking, "Isn't that the purpose of being in a for-profit business?" I can confidently say "no." By serving a purpose well and doing it in a profitable manner, you will make money. The greater, the more needed, and more desired the purpose you choose to serve, the more money you can make.

Profit Leak #7: *Failing to Differentiate Properly*

Does your business strategy encompass a clear value proposition that would be considered an unusual offering and is critical in your target client's buying decision? Are you delivering on the promises embedded in that offering? The answers to these questions may be the primary reasons your sales force hasn't achieved its quotas, your market share hasn't increased, and you've found it increasingly difficult to grow your business.

Profit Leak #8: *Focusing on Tactics Instead of Strategy*
Strategy is about where your company is headed beyond the current year. The tactics you take toward your strategy must be leading you toward accomplishing your strategy. Most leaders just react to the current fires rather than thinking about how to prevent the fires to begin with. Organizations lose lots of time and energy zig-zagging and starting and stopping because leaders don't give enough thought up front to desired outcomes and best paths to achieving them.

Profit Leak #9: *Chasing Revenue Everywhere and Anywhere*
You must identify the kind of customers you want a lot more of. If I analyzed your customer database, it is likely I would find that bad customers (i.e., they pay poorly, are less profitable, complain a lot, are hard to service, do not give referrals, etc.) make up a significant portion of your revenue. This happens mainly because companies find it easier to get the bad customers, particularly when businesses first open and need revenue to survive. In addition, you may mistakenly think that all revenue is good. In practice, it is lack of focus that drains organizational energy and profits. Furthermore, building a base of bad customers creates a wrong brand image and handcuffs your company.

Execution Leaks
Finally, execution leaks are forms of waste in your business. Fixing this issue requires finding the best ways to turn revenue into profit and cash by being efficient with your processes, time, and resources.

Profit Leak #10: *Ineffectively Communicating Your Goals and Expectations*
How effective are you at communicating your goals and expectations? What would happen if I asked everyone on your team to write down the company's goals for the year and, more important, for this month and quarter? Would they

all give me the same answer? Do they know how each of them is expected to contribute to those goals and expectations? Will their answers be specific and measurable? How do you keep them informed of progress?

Profit Leak #11: *Emphasizing the Wrong Priorities and Not Aligning the Team*
If I were to watch you and your team on a weekly basis, would I consider you to be firefighters? Do you spend most of your time discussing and emphasizing the latest daily challenge or big deal opportunity? What proportion of your leadership's time and organization's time is spent on building solutions to propel your company ahead of your competition, to innovate every key process, and to make you better, faster, and cheaper than your competition? How many of your problems continue to recur without leadership ever developing and implementing solutions to make them stop?

Profit Leak #12: *Being Allergic to Saying "No"*
A good strategy makes you say "no" often. Does the way you run your business cause unnecessary complexity in customer service? Does it seem like it takes an act of God for certain decisions to be made? Do you maintain the same rules for all employees in similar circumstances, or do you play favorites? Do you have an open-door policy all the time? Do you say yes to a meeting even though you know it is a waste of time? If so, you aren't saying no enough.

Profit Leak #13: *Monitoring the Wrong Numbers*
Numbers matter. Almost every business recognizes that. However, business leaders often focus their attention on the wrong numbers. As is the case with time management, many companies also do not pay enough attention to goal setting. What's more, many organizations set goals and fail to reach them. To that end, focusing on the right numbers will help you avoid substantial leaks. What is the key weakness in your business model? What is the biggest weakness in your operations? What is causing you not to gain customers? What is causing you to lose customers? What is causing your cost structure to be out of line with your competition's cost structure? Focusing on the right numbers will help you answer each of these questions.

Profit Leak #14: *Holding Ineffective Meetings or Lack of Meetings*
In my experience, the number one complaint of employees everywhere is lack of communication in their company. Communication is one of the most difficult factors to get right. Keys to effective communication are meetings and their frequency. Do your meetings drive follow-through on your annual and quarterly plans? Do they influence consistent results? Do your people find meetings compelling and productive? Do you look forward to having meetings because they are productive, or do you expect them to be a waste of time?

Profit Leak #15: *Failing to Create a Culture of Accountability*
Have you ever wondered why so many annual plans fail? Do you find that your organization fails to achieve its key priorities in its own plan? Trust me when I share with you that you are not alone! If they are honest, most leaders will admit that when they achieve their results, they are often unwilling to show you exactly how. Failing to create a culture of accountability allows your team members to remain unaccountable, which produces profit leaks and a lack of employee efficiency.

Do You Want Your Business to Run at Peak Performance?

Have you identified where the potential leaks are in your business bucket? Here's the first step toward increasing your business success: Accurately identify your leaks and work toward patching the places where your profits are not fully being captured. In my experience, most companies lack the strong leadership operating system and process to help you pull everything together. The evidence is in the leaks.

A strong leadership operating system includes the following aspects:

- You have a process set aside for regular strategic discussion throughout the year.
- Your core values and purpose are alive throughout your organization.
- There is a healthy, aligned leadership team that understands each other's differences and priorities.

- The entire organization is aligned around three to five priorities, with quarterly initiatives to address those priorities.
- There is a communication rhythm established, and information moves through your organization accurately and quickly.
- Every function, position, and financial statement line item has clear accountability, ensuring goals are met.
- A system for collecting and using employee input generates regular input and is causing meaningful changes to your business.
- A system for collecting and using customer feedback and data to improve existing operations and for developing new products and services is functioning well.
- You have an innovation process that ensures you will keep growing long into the future.[13]

Perhaps you think the list above is extreme. As a business and executive coach, I have found that many of the processes I bring to clients are at first perceived as obstacles to getting things done rather than the means to achieving the desired results. And, if implemented in the wrong way, they can be. For example, do you consider concepts like strategic planning, business planning, and meetings to be a waste of your time? Are you the one in the room trying to rush your meetings to get to the point? If so, you have probably never experienced good meetings and effective planning. If you had, they would be permanent rituals in your business!

As we delve deeper into the most common profit leaks, I'd like to mention that they can be found in some companies that have won "Best Place to Work" awards, are on "Fastest-Growing Company" lists, and have won numerous other awards. My point: Just because you have a leak does not make your company a bad company. It just means you are leaving significant money on the table if you choose to ignore it.

PART II
PEOPLE LEAKS

*"Someone is sitting in the shade today because
someone planted a tree a long time ago."*
—Warren Buffett[14]

—— Chapter 5 ——

PROFIT LEAK #1
Poor Leadership

T his may seem like common sense to most business leaders, but poor
leadership creates unbelievably poor results. Earlier in the book, we
discussed the different mindsets most leaders possess. A leader's mindset
greatly impacts the general direction and attitude of the entire company. One
is not necessarily better than the other, but each leadership style and mindset
often comes with its own set of strengths and weaknesses. Many of your team
members may look to you to lead the charge but are left feeling confused or
unsatisfied. These feelings will undoubtedly affect their work product and result
in a substantial profit leak. Steve Jobs said, "Be a yardstick of quality. Some
people aren't used to an environment where excellence is expected."[15] The truth
is that great leadership not only expects success but also creates a culture that
demands it. To expect anything less is just asking for a profit leak.

Gallup, Inc. is well-known for its *State of the American Workplace* report.
From 2010 to 2012 they surveyed 25 million employees in 189 countries and
in 69 languages, asking them their famous 12 questions (provided in Chapter
3) for measuring employee engagement. Essentially, the results showed that only

30 percent of all workers could be referred to as "engaged employees." Engaged employees work with passion and feel a profound connection to their company. They drive innovation and move the organization forward. The scary part of the survey results was that these were the best survey results ever and that these improved statistics were still ugly.

Only 30 Percent of Employees Are Engaged

According to Gallup, essentially 70 percent of today's workforce is being paid to be "not engaged" or "actively disengaged." A staggering 52 percent of employees are "not engaged," meaning they may give you extra effort at times, but they could do that more consistently and have a lot more to offer you and your customers. The remaining 18 percent are "actively disengaged." These employees aren't just unhappy at work, they're busy acting out their unhappiness. Every day, these workers undermine what their engaged coworkers accomplish.

So you have to consider what exactly is causing such a great disconnect. Gallup's findings clearly advanced the notion that leadership is responsible for the 70 percent who are not engaged or actively disengaged. The evidence is supported by the fact that the 70 percent was not spread equally across companies, and there also were differences within the companies. They asserted that the primary difference was to whom those employees reported. When employees you have invested in are not engaged, you get less return on your investment. In other words, for every dollar you spend in salary, you are likely getting 50 percent or less of the productivity you are paying for unless you have skilled leaders to keep them engaged.[16]

How Are You Measuring Leader Performance?

Now you have no choice but to ask some very important questions: Do you have any poor leaders? How are you measuring the performance of your leaders? I find it baffling that while the largest salaries in companies go to leaders, they are the people who are measured and held accountable the least! Ask yourself whether you've set two or three key performance indicators that each of your leaders is responsible for improving. When they don't take those important steps, do you fire them? Do you focus on the goals, or how they are even achieved? In reality, you probably do not. It is easy to hire what we perceive to be great leaders and then shift our attention elsewhere, assuming they will simply get the job done. But there is no justification for that belief.

A clear example of this problem is illustrated by a discussion I had with a client who is a CEO. We talked about the chief financial officer of his midmarket company. He said his CFO was great, an "A" player in fact. The CEO likes this person because he works hard, cares about the company, and is intellectually smart. He says the right things, comes from a great background, has all the appropriate certifications, and provides sound financial counsel. However, all the CEO had described was the basic requirements and expectations for any CFO. This particular CFO was not really excelling in any area. He maintained the status quo and got the job done . . . albeit barely.

The CEO ignored the fact that his CFO was only performing in one aspect of his job! The CEO did not pay attention to numerous aspects of leadership lacking in this CFO, including:

- The CFO had consistently failed for an entire year to deliver on any of the personal priorities he'd established and agreed to during each quarterly planning process.
- It consistently took forty-five days from month's end to close the books. In other words, the management team was relying on outdated financial data to make its decisions.
- The entire team reporting to the CFO had been identified as poor performers and did not live the core values of the company. He had done nothing to replace any of them, even after acknowledging that they were not performing and having to compensate for their lack of performance.
- On more than one occasion, the CEO had been forced to create analytics on his own that would normally be created by accounting because he could not depend on the CFO or the accounting department to get it done.
- The CFO consistently made comments implying that he was smarter than everyone else in meetings. In many cases, he was condescending.

- The CFO struggled with understanding things from other people's point of view. Worse, he did not see a need to do so.
- When others made valuable contributions in meetings, he would demean the importance of their comments.
- His team members did not care for him and only tolerated him because they had to. As result, they would try to avoid him when making critical decisions rather than seek him out for his financial acumen.

By allowing a poor leader to continue, a CEO effectively communicates that the inept person designated to lead has more to offer than everyone else put together, which is always a poor choice. The number one priority as a leader must be to get, keep, and grow a team of people who perform at levels that exceed your competition. It is a best practice to measure your leaders' performance on the dimensions of recruiting, coaching, developing, motivating, and nurturing people! If you measure those leaders by the wrong things, you shouldn't then expect the right behaviors.

Alignment is key to the overall accomplishment of business goals. To help with this, ensure that individual leaders report to the CEO to demonstrate that their group's objectives are consistently aligned with those of the business. This approach will support the notion that the entire team is moving in the right direction.

Inept leaders cause everyone around them to perform at lower levels, and you then lose access to a lot of great ideas. People are less apt to willingly give extra effort when they feel it either won't be noticed or doesn't even matter in the first place. So if you have a leader on your team who is not able to get top performances out of his or her team, stop harassing the front-line people and address your real issue: leadership.

Do Your Leaders Have What It Takes to Influence Others?

A key measurement of a great leader is his or her ability to positively influence people to work together toward mutually beneficial results. Being smart, knowing an industry, working hard, having good communication skills, and being able to get things done all make for a good team member, but many times do not produce a great leader. Too often, these attributes are the qualities given the most weight when companies are picking leaders. Fact is, most people can be good workers but will never be good leaders.

When you seek to hire or promote someone into a leadership role, you need to focus on whether and how he or she will influence others. A great way to measure a potential leader is to see if they can lead without authority.

Five Questions to Ask When Promoting or Hiring Your Next Leader:

1. Does this person possess and have the ability to communicate vision?
2. Does he/she influence his/her peers, and in what ways?
3. Do his/her peers feel comfortable discussing issues with him/her?
4. Do his/her peers look at him/her as a voice on their behalf?
5. Does this person use authority to get others to accomplish goals?

Often, you will find great leaders have ample amounts of moral character traits that include respect, gratitude, compassion, and integrity. They challenge others to greatness and possess performance character traits that include curiosity, humility, vision, self-control, drive and passion.[17]

What Actions Can Be Taken?

Leaders are responsible for people, functional roles, and processes. You need to set your leaders up for success. Accomplish this by clarifying the following for every leader in the organization:

1. Expectations that the primary responsibility of a leader is to coach, mentor, and nurture an environment where employees stay motivated and do their best work.
2. Give moral character traits equal weight to performance character traits when evaluating performance.[18]
3. Where the company is headed.
4. Long- and short-term goals to be achieved. These are the measurable outcomes that would not happen if their position did not exist.

5. Key people and processes for which they are responsible.

6. Key performance indicators for established goals.

7. Patterns of behavior that inhibit success and provide coaching to help your leaders address those behaviors that are hindering their success.

Most importantly you must nurture an environment that fosters leaders!

Key Chapter Points
Profit Leak #1: *Poor Leadership*

- Poor leadership creates unbelievably poor results.
- According to Gallup, essentially 70 percent of today's workforce is being paid to be "not engaged" or "actively disengaged."
  - A staggering 52 percent of employees are "not engaged," meaning they may give you extra effort at times, but they could do that more consistently and have a lot more to offer you and your customers.
  - The remaining 18 percent are "actively disengaged."
- Gallup asserted that the primary difference between 30 percent that were "actively engaged" and the rest was to whom those employees reported.
  - This is important because when employees you have invested in are not engaged, you get less return on your investment.
  - In other words, for every dollar you spend in salary, you are likely getting 50 percent or less of the productivity you are paying for unless you have skilled leaders to keep them engaged.
- Every leader must have two or three key performance indicators that measure how effective they are as "leaders."
- The number one priority as a leader must be to get, keep, and grow a team of people who perform at levels that exceed that of your competition.
- Inept leaders cause everyone around them to perform at lower levels, and you then lose access to a lot of great ideas.
- Being smart, knowing an industry, working hard, having good communication skills, and being able to get things done all make for a good team member, but many times do not produce a great leader.

- When you seek to hire or promote someone into a leadership role, focus on whether and how he or she will influence others.
- The primary responsibility of a leader is to provide vision and to coach, mentor, and nurture an environment where employees can stay motivated and do their best work.
- Great leaders have ample amounts of moral character traits that include respect, gratitude, compassion, and integrity.
- Great leaders challenge others to greatness and possess performance character traits that include curiosity, humility, vision, self-control, drive and passion.
- Give moral character traits equal weight to performance character traits when evaluating performance.
- You must nurture an environment that fosters leaders.

Chapter 6

PROFIT LEAK #2
"B" and "C" Players

In the previous chapter, we discussed how important leadership is to your company's overall success. There is no arguing with that. But even great leadership cannot overcome the limited abilities of "B" or "C" talent. Often, leaders can only go as far as those they lead. Think about it from a coaching perspective. You could have a world-class coach, but if you have a team of goofy players with mediocre athletic ability, you'll only get so far. At the end of the day, the coach can draw up all the plays he wants, but the team has to execute them on the playing field. Players have to act to make split-second decisions and make the plays as the game unfolds. The players determine whether you win or lose. Business is no different.

It has been said that a great leader is like a gardener who plants seeds, makes sure that the soil has the right nutrients, and then nurtures the soil. The gardener cannot grow his crops, he can only provide the right conditions for growth and provide the right seeds. Great leadership puts a person in a position to excel and succeed, but that person still has to do all the heavy lifting.[19]

Trust me when I say it is imperative to have A-rated talent to obtain optimal results. Then it takes leadership to keep them at that level. Now don't think this profit leak is about rating people. Rather, this leak is about establishing the standards by which you choose your team and to which you hold your team accountable. Bad hiring and accountability practices, not putting people in the right seats where they can excel, failure to hold people accountable to key outcomes, and weakness in your culture represent poor leadership.

One of the biggest profit leaks in your company may be related to your philosophy regarding personnel. The biggest cost in most companies is payroll; therefore, your biggest asset or investment is people. How seriously are you and your company taking this investment, and how disciplined are you in demanding that it produces an adequate standard of performance?

What Are "A" Players?

"A" players are employees who consistently meet productivity requirements (performance standards) and consistently live your company's core values. Your productivity requirements should be set at a high bar and be readily achievable. Do not set the bar so high that it takes a unicorn to fill your position. Regardless of the role, strong performers can produce at two to three times the output of their peers. Many organizations, however, label the wrong people as their "A" players. You may be favoring people you can identify with more personally, that you have less conflict with, who have organizational tenure, who have the most institutional or industry knowledge, or that you consider loyal to you. They are not necessarily "A" players. If you are like many leaders, you may be giving more weight to only the few attributes or qualities you find important. Unfortunately, those may or may not be critical to the real mission, purpose, or success of the position.[20]

I had a client who had an issue with his controller and was leaning toward dismissal. This was a sales culture, and the CEO favored people who were outgoing and communicative. He felt the controller did not fit his culture. The controller was reclusive and preferred to work in a quiet place where she could concentrate. Also this controller was not afraid to tell the CEO when the company was wasting money, even if it was the CEO doing so. The controller was very focused on precision and getting things right. She often voiced concerns when other leaders would exaggerate their points or make decisions with no supporting data.

The CEO failed to realize the issues he had with the controller were not related to her skills and talents. Instead, they were related to her behavioral style, which was different from the CEO's. The controller's behavioral style helped balance out the leadership team and was essential to her being a good controller. Being the decisive and outgoing communicator that the CEO preferred was not an essential quality for being an effective controller. The controller actually lived all of the core values of the business perfectly. As a matter of fact, everything produced by the department was helpful, timely, and accurate. Moreover, she treated the company as if its assets were her own, and she protected the owners.

So what should cause someone to be categorized as a "B" or "C" player? A "B" player consistently lives all of your organization's core values but is not meeting 100 percent of their position's productivity requirements. A "B/C" player performs at the required levels but does not consistently demonstrate one or more core values. "C" players are failing to meet the performance *and* values standards. In all cases, anyone who is *not* classified as "A" should only be kept on your team if management believes they can become "A" players with proper training and coaching within an acceptable period of time. If not, the best thing you can do is to speedily replace them.

Proper Use of Employee Performance Classifications

Classify employees to identify leaks in your bucket, or to quantify the gaps between required and actual performance. Do not classify them to label them or brand them. This happens all too often. Your process must identify the gaps and force a discussion on how to address each employee's circumstance in the appropriate manner so that the leak is closed.

To truly analyze the type of team members you have, you must understand the proper use of performance classifications systems. If these systems are misused, you could cause good performers to decline or not improve by failing to offer them the proper training, coaching, feedback, and measuring tools. You could also negatively affect your culture by overweighting or underweighting certain team members. Classification errors become obvious if you elevate the wrong person to a position of leadership.

Ultimately, classification aims to create positive action by helping a person find a role in your company where he or she can achieve peak performance; by creating an environment and circumstances where that person performs at peak performance; by removing obstacles to peak performance; by identifying the people who do not fit your culture and removing them; and by understanding what needs to be done to help someone perform at a proper level of productivity. Everyone performs at a "B" level sometimes, but it is our job as leaders to help lead employees get back to A-player status as quickly as possible.

Eight Questions to Ask When Someone Does Not Perform at an "A" Level:

1. Have you properly communicated to the person what is expected of them?
2. Has this person been an "A" player in the past? If so, what has changed?
3. Does the person have the skills and knowledge necessary to perform his or her job at a high level?
4. What training is required to get this person to peak performance?
5. Has the organization created unnecessary barriers to this person becoming successful?
6. Do you believe this person will achieve productivity within a reasonable amount of time?
7. Does this person believe in your core values, and is he or she willing to live them?
8. Which processes, if fixed, would lead to better success in the future?

Answering these questions will help you diagnose the issue(s). Sometimes team members are well past the rebound zone. That is, you simply cannot resuscitate their performance. Other times, with a little redirection and emphasis on coaching, mentoring, or training, an "A" player who is underperforming can bounce back. Either way, you have to determine the exact problem and then take great strides to address it.

Why is the "B" and "C" Performance Issue Not Really Being Addressed?

The primary reason that employees are permitted to underperform is a lack of clarity in leadership. Leaders are often too busy doing their own jobs to focus enough time and energy on what they really want from their team. And when they have a good idea of exactly what they desire, often they do not effectively communicate it. Even then, performance is often not being measured in a way that allows a person to be held accountable.

Most sharp business owners do measure the performance of their businesses on at least a monthly basis, but then they fail to properly relate that measurement back to individual employee performance. By not requiring a specific level of performance, monitoring that performance, and holding employees accountable, you are allowing your employees to establish their own performance requirements. Common sense tells me your employees will set lower work standards for themselves than you would.

You may be wondering how "B" and "C" performances can cost a company millions and go unnoticed and unaddressed. The primary reason: There is no financial statement line item to quantify the cost of the lost customers, lost productivity, mistakes, and lost opportunities attributable to these nonperforming players. This begs the question: Why would you ever even consider keeping a "B" or "C" player?

When Do You Keep "B" or "C" Players?

Keep a "B" or "C" player when you confidently believe they will become an "A" player within a reasonable amount of time. If you cannot define how and when that will occur, stop fooling yourself and cut the cord. With that said, you may have to keep a person on board until his or her replacement is found because having a vacancy will be too disruptive to the business.

Leaders have lots of excuses for not replacing their "B" or "C" players. All of the reasons boil down to either leadership laziness or just plain poor leadership.

Let's again clarify the definition of the "A" player. They are not extraordinary. They are people who meet the requirements of their positions and fit your culture. Anything less, and you did not get what you paid for.

Every company leader I have met who had a cash flow problem or was unsatisfied with their growth or profits also had a people problem. Growth problems attributable to bad strategy are also people problems because companies that choose the right people (including advisors, consultants, and coaches) are less likely to have strategy problems. Think about it. The employees of any business are like the cogs that keep a machine running. Doesn't it make sense that the machine won't operate at optimum performance when you have broken, incorrect, or rusty pieces inside of it?

I have yet to meet with a company that already had the processes in place to allow them to demonstrate that at least 75 percent of their employees were "A" players. Many initially believed they had 75 percent or more, but that was basically a wish and a prayer, as they were not tracking any performance indicators to prove their people were performing. In fact, most had 40 percent or even less.

Research shows that replacing even one "B" or "C" player with an "A" player has a big impact on a business. Some companies misunderstand what could happen if they commit to doing what it takes to move toward achieving A-player performance in every position in their company. They create walls or personal obstacles, some of which sound like this:

- There are not enough "A" players out there.
- It will take much longer to hire people.
- It is too complicated.
- It takes too much manpower.
- It can't happen in our industry.
- I have to fire everyone who is a "B" and" C" player.
- "A" players must be paid more than "B" and "C" players.

The truth is that these are all myths and limiting beliefs, allowing leadership to continue to justify poor hiring practices and maintain the status quo.

The Container Store provides one of the best examples of how to build an organization with "A" players. I was fortunate to hear Kip Tindell, founder of The Container Store, share his formula for building a great organization. He built his company from a small start-up to one of the most respected businesses around. With the help of his "A" player mantra, his company is still growing at 20 percent a year and has done so since inception. His formula has five important keys to success:

1. *Pay.* They pay 50 percent to 100 percent above industry average. Tindell knew one great person could do the work of two to three average people. "A" players pay for their "extra" salary threefold, so overall labor costs are actually lower than the competition's. His people are extremely proud to be part of the company and of their performance.

2. *Recruiting and Retention.* To win, he knew he must only hire great people. He knew "A" players only like to work with other "A" players. They do not want to be surrounded by mediocrity. They would choose to be in his company to be on a great team. This means his recruiting process had to be phenomenal to find and select the right people and never settle. They wanted more of the best and brightest out of school. They've been rewarded with less than 10 percent turnover in an industry that typically experiences over 100 percent turnover.

3. *Training and Onboarding.* Tindell provides eighty-four hours of formal training in the first year compared to the industry average, which is eight hours.

4. *Real transparency and communication.* Your leaders and managers can thrive with clear communication and transparency. If they don't feel fully informed, they feel left out, and their performance will suffer.

5. *Culture.* Culture is everything. Free the employees to choose the means to the ends, but tell them the foundational principles to use in making those decisions. All employees will give you 25 percent of their efforts, considered to be the bare minimum amount of productivity required to keep your job. To get the other 75 percent, they have to love their manager and culture.[21]

In each of these steps, you'll quickly come to a singular conclusion: Great leaders invest enormous time and energy into their team. They create a culture that not only invites in "A" players, but also demands an A-level performance.

What Actions Can Be Taken?

What steps can you take to build a high-performance organization? Just like any machine that takes proper maintenance and care to run smoothly, repairs are costly when problems are ignored. So likely we can all agree it is much more efficient and cost effective to ward off those repairs. People already spend enormous amounts of time interviewing candidates. They need to learn the right techniques and processes to determine whether the people they interview are the right choices for the positions. The real challenge is instilling an organization-wide commitment to high-performance standards, and practice makes perfect.

There is no one-size-fits-all sort of remedy. Different companies require different solutions. Always remember you're dealing with real people and real problems, so do not remove the compassion from the equation. Just because someone is classified as "C" or "B" in his or her current role does not mean he or she cannot become an "A" player in another position or possibly in their existing position, with just a little more training.

It has been said, "That which gets measured gets done!"[22] When measurement tools are put in place, leaders are shocked by how many employees are placed under the categories of "B" and "C" players. This performance gap costs companies millions in profit leaks. You can take several process steps, however, to resuscitate and improve your organizational productivity.

Six Steps to A-Player Status:

1. For each position in your company, identify two to three key performance indicators that the person in the position has direct control over and would prove they are performing well in their job. Establish a high but realistic standard for each indicator.

2. Communicate these indicators and the standards to the person in the position and then measure actual performance versus the standards you've set.

3. Establish a process for constantly reinforcing your core values with all of your employees.

4. On a quarterly basis, review how consistently each member of your team lives your core values and meets the performance expectations of their role

5. Put employees who are not living your core values or meeting performance expectations on very specific performance plans designed to direct them toward achieving desired performance.

6. Take immediate action to help employees who are not meeting their requirements, and those who cannot meet your standards should be considered for replacement.

Key Chapter Points:
Profit Leak #2: *"B" and "C" Players*

- How well your employees make decisions and act on the front lines determine how profitable and fast a company grows.
  - Great leadership cannot overcome the limited abilities of "B" or "C" talent.
- Bad hiring and accountability practices, not putting people in the seats where they can excel, and failure to hold them accountable to key outcomes are the results of poor leadership.
- The biggest cost in most companies is payroll; therefore, your biggest asset or investment is people.
  - How serious are you and your company taking this investment, and how disciplined are you in demanding that it produces an adequate standard of performance?
- "A" players are employees who consistently meet the productivity requirements (performance standards) of their positions and consistently live your company's core values.
- Anyone who is not classified as A should only be kept on your team if management believes they can become "A" players with proper training and coaching within an acceptable period of time.

- You are already paying every one of your employees to be an "A" player.
- Your productivity requirements should be set at a high bar and be readily achievable by everyone.
- Regardless of the role, strong performers can produce at two to three times the output of their peers.
- Classification aims to create positive action by helping a person find a role in your company where he or she can achieve peak performance; to create an environment and circumstances where that person can maintain peak performance; to remove obstacles to peak performance; to identify and remove the people who do not fit your culture; and to recognize what needs to be done to help someone perform at a proper level of productivity.
- Ask the eight questions when someone is not performing at an "A" level.
- By not requiring a specific level of performance, monitoring that performance, and holding employees accountable, you are allowing your employees to establish their own performance requirements.
- Every company leader I have met who had a cash flow problem or was unsatisfied with their growth or profits also had a people problem.
- Practice the Six Steps to "A" Player Status.

---| *Chapter 7* |---

PROFIT LEAK #3:
Financial Transparency

G reat leaders are familiar with the intimate details of their respective businesses. And there is no better measurement of a company's health and well-being than its finances. More than anything, your firm's financial health ought to be at the forefront of your consideration when it comes to detecting leaks. Your financial statements must tell a very realistic and accurate story about your company's health. They should provide a crystal-clear view of whether you are prospering or drowning, succeeding or failing. If you crunch the numbers and are still unclear, that is an entirely different problem. For now, let's discuss the third profit leak, as financial transparency inspires higher expectations.

You Need to Understand Your Financial Statements

While I am a CPA, accounting is not my passion. I did practice accounting and finance for approximately 15 years and am grateful for the knowledge I gained. Quite frankly, many leaders depend too much on their CFOs, controllers, accountants, and bookkeepers and really need to get a better handle on what their financial statements mean and what really influences their results. If they did, they would demand more, invest more in their financial departments, and even upgrade some people. I am not here to teach you about financial statements, but I do want to make sure you walk away with a few principles that are critical to know to help you improve your business:

- **Revenue is vanity, profit is sanity, and cash is king!**

  There are two financial statement line items (assuming you have reconciled your books) that are not estimates: cash and debt. A sign of a healthy business model is that it spins off lots of cash. If you are not producing cash, you need to quickly figure out how to get to a positive cash model. Failure to do so will ultimately result in debt. Few businesses successfully avoid needing to use any debt.

  One form of acquiring debt occurs when someone invests in your company and receives an equity ownership interest. We do not normally refer to this as debt, but do not fool yourself—it *is* debt. In fact, it is very expensive debt that comes with a lot of strings attached. It is a debt with ownership attached. While we do not want to get into the depths of this, a lot of research has proven that there is an inverse relationship between success and companies that have taken on early private equity. *Fast Company* magazine published a great article on this titled "Why Most Venture-Backed Companies Fail." In the article, written by Faisal Hogue, Hogue identifies as many as 75 percent of the venture-backed companies in the study that never returned cash to investors, with 30 percent to 40 percent of those liquidating assets, causing investors to lose all of their money. His findings are based on research into more than 2,000 venture-backed companies that raised at least $1 million from 2004 to 2010. [23] In other words, your company is likely to fail if it takes on private equity too early.

  The takeaway: Too many leaders use debt to create bad business models and practices. The best way to succeed in business is to force yourself to bootstrap, learn how to attract enough revenue, and get your customers to fund your business.

You *will* go bankrupt if your business model does not produce enough cash. Period! As a general rule of thumb, there are two acceptable occasions for taking on debt:

1. Asset Leverage—Leveraging an asset that produces a high return on investment as part of your business model.

2. Fund Extraordinary Growth—A business with an exceptional return on capital (higher than the cost equity and debt capital combined) trying to capture market share before the competitors catch on.

In too many cases, business owners cannot clearly articulate how their business will produce an exceptional cash model and then end up burning through tons of cash. Most of their assumptions are essentially wishes and prayers because they have no tangible action plans showing the path. They do not even understand their cash model. They are just excited about their product or service. Many leaders use gross profit margin or EBITDA (earnings before interest, taxes, depreciation, and amortization) to determine whether they are doing well. But you must look at your entire financial picture because in many cases EBITDA is nowhere close to cash.

• **1 + 1 + 1 ≠ 3**

To get a lot of value out of this book, you will need to be open-minded. So let's show you how a basic addition problem does not work when you are focusing on improving your financial statements. Hopefully you can suspend other preconceived notions as you continue reading. Please print out the most recent full-year income statement for your company and do the following:

1. Calculate a **1% increase in revenue**

2. Write that number next to revenue.

3. Add that number to your revenue to get a new revenue amount.

4. Calculate a **1% reduction in cost of goods sold (CGS).**

5. Write that number next to cost of goods sold (CGS).

6. Subtract that number from cost of goods sold to get the new **CGS** amount.

7. Now subtract the new **cost of goods sold** amount from the new **revenue** amount.
8. The result will be your new **gross margin**.
9. Calculate a **1% reduction in selling, general, and administrative expenses (SGA) as a % of revenue**.
10. Write the number next to **SGA**.
11. Now subtract that result from **SGA** to get a new amount.
12. Now subtract the new **SGA** amount from the new **Gross Margin** amount.
13. The result is your new **net profit**.
14. Divide the new **net profit** by the old **net profit** and subtract 1.
15. The result is your growth rate in **net profit**.

1 + 1 + 1 = A Lot More Than 3

Revenue	11,288,000	Increase 1%	11,400,880	1%
Cost of Goods Sold	1,634,000		1,539,119	
% of Revenue	14.50%	Reduce 1%	13.50%	1%
Gross Margin	9,654,000		9,861,761	
Selling General & Administrative	8,846,000		8,820,861	
% of Revenue	78.37%	Reduce 1%	77.37%	1%
Net Profit	808,000		1,040,900	29%

As you can see from this example, 1 percent improvements in revenue, gross margin, and reducing your selling, general and administrative expenses increase this client's profit margin by 29 percent. This exercise usually results in increases of somewhere between 25 and 35 percent.

The lesson here: You only need to make small changes to your business to have large impacts to profit and cash. You cannot make those changes if you do not understand your financial statements.

- **Improving the Cash Model**

  People make financial statements overly complex. By applying a little focus, though, you can improve it every month. Every business has the same six to eight levers. Ask yourself the same eight questions constantly (remember the power of 1 above):

  1. Price: Are we bundling and offering our products and services in a way that allows us to maximize price? In other words, can you increase price?
  2. Sales Volume: What can you do to increase volume?
  3. Reduce Direct Costs of Cost of Goods/Services Sold as a % of Revenue: How can third parties, technology, process, different materials, and logistics help you lower the variable costs required to offer your products and services?
  4. Reduce Overhead as a % of Revenue: How can you lower your cost of acquiring customers, reduce administrative overhead burden, and other indirect costs to providing products and services?
  5. Receivables: How can you collect money from customers faster?
  6. Payables: How can you slow payments to your vendors and employees without damaging your relationships?
  7. Inventory: How can you reduce the amount of inventory required to support your business and speed up the number of turns?
  8. Capital Costs: How do you lower your costs of debt and equity?[24]

- **View Expenses as Investments**

  The concept of expenses causes a dilemma for many decision makers. Depending on your level of optimism you either spend with no concern for the consequences, or you focus too much on the fact that you are spending money. Most often it is the latter. When you're focused on how much something will cost rather than on what you will get for your investment, you are missing the whole purpose for the expenditure. For example, a common expense decision is adding a position in your company. You may focus more on what you have paid for the position in the past or on what others have indicated is proper pay for the position. The real inquiry revolves around what the right person could accomplish in the position, as well as the compensation required to attract such a person in current market conditions. Many companies have trouble finding the right people to fill their positions because the compensation they offer is not attractive to the caliber of candidate they want to hire.

The best example is how most leaders approach their investments related to technology. These investments must be viewed in three categories: 1) mandatory: hardware, maintenance, servers, break fix, and security to support decisions already made; 2) operational efficiency and scalability; and 3) industry disruption/research and development. In all cases you have a responsibility to invest wisely. It is all about value. Buyer beware, as you get what you pay for. You job is to achieve the desired outcome with the minimum investment. This is where I see most leaders go wrong. They look at the expenditures and not the outcomes.

In the first category, how much revenue and profit does it cost you if your systems are down for any period of time, or if your employees cannot be productive because their computers do not work? What does it cost you if they are spending time fixing their computers and finding and installing software for themselves rather than doing what they were really hired to do?

My biggest concern in the second category is technology. Leaders regularly invest in technology claiming it will make them more efficient and scalable. In other words, they intend to increase speed, add efficiency, and reduce labor intensity so that their cost structure can change. More often than many want to admit, no such benefits occur. Inadequate key performance indicators were determined, benefits were never tracked, and in many cases the organization increased costs rather than lowering them. It is likely your company has invested heavily in technology only to find you are still trying to discover your productivity gains. The only firms profiting appear to be the technology companies providing the products and services. Worse, you cannot pass on the added costs to your customers.

The third category is often confused with the second category. Many times we are tinkering with very technological ventures, calling them strategic and not recognizing them as tactical efficiency ideas. When these ventures don't work, we justify them as research and development. However, they really do not belong in this category. Unless the benefits you are going after will transform your industry and business model, your investment does not belong in this category.

- **Understand the Difference Between Variable and Fixed Costs**
  Break your costs down between fixed and variable expenses. Variable expenses are costs that are expected to move in direct correlation to revenue. They include personnel, material, and other inputs that are directly related to providing your product or service. Fixed expenses are everything else, and over the course of time we look to gain leverage. Your fixed costs should not grow at the same rate as revenue. At different intervals of growth, you will need to increase your fixed costs at a rate faster than revenue to prepare for your next stage of growth, but then those fixed costs should be spread over much larger amounts of revenue, thus becoming a smaller percentage of revenue.

  Do not assume all fixed costs are really fixed. Understand how much is discretionary. In other words, you may have some extra people you could possibly eliminate if things were tight, perks and benefits that are nice but not necessary (e.g., season tickets to see your favorite NBA team), and tasks that can be done in different ways. For example, you could use third parties to provide information technology and other support services rather than having it all in-house. In some cases, companies find they can outsource certain functions to increase quality and service while dramatically reducing cost.

Putting It All Together

You know you and your leadership team understand the financial statements when you start making priority decisions because of them. For example, consider a manufacturing company that prioritized based on a leader's knowledge of the financials. At a top level, the company thought they were doing great! They experienced a 50 percent revenue growth in the last year, and the company had maintained its net profit percentage from the previous one. The company was on track to enjoy just shy of $10 million in revenue and believed they would easily break $12 million by the new year.

The leadership team learned how to read their financials just in time! You see, even in light of all this perceived success, they were actually at risk of insolvency. They had a bad financial model and did not realize the gravity of their situation. To generate the increase in revenue, they had added a new revenue stream. This new customer profile changed their business and financial model, causing inventory to increase from $400,000 the previous year to $1.6 million in the current one. While you would expect inventory to increase along with revenue, that was simply not the case here. They learned their collections had slowed, so while their income statement showed $9.9 million in revenue, they had collected just $9.1 million. The impact of the new business model meant that while they generated $9.9 million in revenue, they actually generated $687,000 in **negative** operating cash flow. To make matters worse, they invested $560,000 in new assets to support their growth. **So over the course of 12 months this particular business generated $1.247 million in negative cash flows.**

Armed with this knowledge, in one planning session they used what they learned about 1 + 1 + 1 to improve cash flows on an annualized rate of $2.6 million. They did this through focusing on:

- Price. They determined a 1 percent price increase was worth $88,500 in cash flow. They believed they could methodically increase pricing by 2 percent across their product line for a total improvement of $177,000.
- Volume. Based on current customers, new customers, new products they were prepared to launch, and reasonable increases in new customers, they believed volume could easily increase by 15 percent. Each percentage point was worth $45,500, for a total cash flow improvement of $682,500.
- Cost of Sales. They evaluated how they were managing labor and knew they were very inefficient. In addition, they were not doing a good job of

buying materials in bulk. The combination of these two initiatives had the capacity to improve margin by at least $516,000.

- Overhead. After reviewing their overhead, they knew they had added people too quickly without seeing a return on their investment. They were going to cut back in some areas, invest in others, and expect overhead as a percentage of revenue to drop by 4 percentage points for a cash flow improvement of $217,000.

- Inventory. Immediately, they put processes in place to properly manage and control inventory. These controls were expected to reduce inventory by 59 days, improving cash flow by $649,000.

- Receivables. By hiring a higher-caliber accounts receivables person, the business believed it could reduce the number of outstanding days by 15 to improve cash flow by $405,000.

After six months of focusing on these initiatives, this company improved cash flow by $1.5 million and also eliminated all debt from its balance sheet.

Transparency Equals Results

You may have heard the phrase "That which is measurable can be improved." The business above provides a great example of how important transparency can be to a company's overall health. These fundamental principles are crucial to creating the transparency required by every business in existence. To improve your financial health, you have to be clear on its current state. If you are blind to the numbers and unable to obtain a crystal-clear understanding of your current diagnosis, your prognosis will likely be inaccurate. Frankly, your business will never reach optimal health or have the ability to rebound when it hits the skids. Transparency lets you evaluate where you stand and where you need to improve.

Once you understand this on an internal level, you will then be able to project this on an external level and to your team. Your team will then be in a better position to refine their practices and focus on areas that need improvement. They can only do that if and when they are clear on where the leaks reside. You can't just make statements like, "We are losing money, and expenses are out of control," or "We need to figure out how to cut costs" without determining the actual source of the leaks.

As leaders, we all want to inspire higher expectations in our team. When your team members and team leaders can truly see how cash rich the company is, they will likely remain focused and inspired to truly keep it up. If they happen to see books reflective of unhealthy practices, likely they will comprehend their company and jobs are on the line, which will motivate everyone to come together and right the ship. This is why transparency is so important and also why financial indiscretion or financial silence can negatively impact your company. You are all in this together, so use your books as a way to motivate and inspire your company. Only then will teamwork be directed toward preventing the financial leaks that come with being outside of the circle of financial information.

Key Chapter Points:
Profit Leak #3: *Financial Transparency*

- Your financial statements must tell a very realistic and accurate story about your company's health.
- Financial transparency inspires higher expectations.
- Every leader needs to understand how they influence financial results.
- Revenue is vanity, profit is sanity, and cash is king! A sign of a healthy business model is that it spins off lots of cash.
- Seventy-five percent of the venture-backed companies never returned cash to investors, with 30 percent to 40 percent of those liquidating assets, causing investors to lose all of their money.
- As a general rule of thumb, there are two acceptable occasions for taking on debt: leveraging assets and funding extraordinary growth. On the latter, remember the caveat about funding the exceptional cash model.
- $1 + 1 + 1 \neq 3$. You only need to make small changes to your business to have large impacts to profit and cash.
- The eight ways to improve your cash flow model involve pricing, volume, reducing cost of sales, reducing and controlling overhead, collecting faster, paying bills slower, reducing your cost of capital, and

increasing inventory levels and speed. Remember the eight questions to ask constantly.

- View expenses as investments. When you're focused on how much something will cost rather than on what you will get for your investment, you are missing the whole purpose for the expenditure.

- Your fixed costs should not grow at the same rate as revenue. At different intervals of growth, increase your fixed costs at a rate faster than revenue to prepare for your next stage of growth, but then that fixed cost should be spread over much larger amounts of revenue, thus becoming a smaller percentage of revenue.

- Use transparency to drive results. Transparency lets you evaluate where you stand and where you need to improve.

Chapter 8

PROFIT LEAK #4
Vacant Positions

E
arlier in the book, we addressed the value of hiring a strong team. Create an organization of "A" players, and you'll be on the fast track to success. But when it comes to your team, profit leaks aren't always caused by hiring the wrong people or by having "B" and "C" players. Sometimes profit leaks happen because people are not in the right place or not in place at all. Likely, you've invested the largest part of your budget in your people, and investing it the wrong way can create one of the biggest leaks in your bucket. Many leaders suffer from tunnel vision; they become too focused on individual salaries and myopic when staffing their company. While cost management is important for businesses, it may also become a trap, causing you to inadvertently develop leaks in growth and profits. Do you give enough consideration to how hiring the right people can bring value to and help you grow your business?

In just nine months, one of our clients increased revenue by 70 percent by identifying where they had failed to fill and underinvested in positions. The company was growing and profitable but could not turn profits into cash fast enough. Had they continued with inadequate staffing, they might have gone insolvent. Instead, they invested in growing their team and found that cash flow exploded. Only when you invest wisely can you maximize your return on investment.

Imagine your business as a sports team. If we tried to match your team against the competition on a player-by-player, position-by-position basis, how ready is your organization to compete? How does it affect your team when you do not have the right structure? How does it affect the team when one of the positions is not filled properly because the owner is trying to keep payroll down? How does it affect the team when an "A" player has to leave their "real" position to make up for the absence or inadequacy of another player? How well can your team perform when it has only filled some of its positions and has to compete against another team that has a full roster? What happens when one player has too many positions to cover? What happens when an "A" player has to play too many minutes and the other team's player has had plenty of rest? You probably have an idea what these answers may look like, but nonetheless, let's take some time to explore each of these questions.

Don't Fall Victim to Organizational Mismatch

We work with many companies that have experienced significant growth in a short time, and frequently these companies suffer from organizational mismatch. Basically, this means they have the wrong people with the wrong skillsets in the wrong positions. We also find many situations where some people are responsible for too many roles and therefore perform few, if any of them, particularly well. Leaks can be created in either of these scenarios. But let's dive a little deeper and consider how organizational mismatch can be the result of one (or all) of the following reasons:

1. **Growth**. When a company experiences rapid growth it is common to find the leaders scrambling to fill necessary roles and either hiring the first available candidates or filling the positions with current employees who "know the business." Essentially, they "plug holes" with people instead of hiring the right people for the right roles.

2. **Overconfidence**. In the midst of growth, leaders may believe their team could simply "pull it together and make it happen," no matter what. The company shifts people around or asks people to pull double duty because it seems like the easiest solution.

3. **Comfort.** Leaders mistakenly think they can shuffle top performers from one position into another. Past success in one position equals proficiency in another, right? Wrong.

4. **Lack of Organizational Planning.** Leaders spend more time working in the business rather than on directing the business. The executive teams need to step back and really understand what organizational structure will help them win in the long term. Instead, leaders keep addressing the current fires without developing the foresight to prevent fires from occurring to begin with.

Let's talk about the key questions we find many leaders do not address quickly enough, and how they can create big Leaky Buckets.

Do You Have the Right Structure to Win?

Is your structure evolving with your company's growth? Is your structure properly designed to support both your internal and external strategy? In other words, do you have the structure best designed to serve your ideal prospects' problems better than any of your competitors? Are you set up to acquire those ideal customers?

In most cases, businesses are very focused on products and services, yet their structure has been formed by accident rather than by design. Typically, this results in failing to see where your structure is causing unnecessary complexity, underinvesting in critical roles, and lacking in accountability. For example, the CFO of an organization failed to see the critical importance of adding the human resources function to the company's organizational structure. Rather than invest $75,000 in this one essential position and $90,000 to engage a qualified consultant to set up procedures and help in hiring the new director, the CFO opted to spread the responsibilities for human resources among numerous unqualified people in the organization.

Failing to have a trained human resources manager cost the business $1.6 million. The organization was growing rapidly and had to replace a number of "B" and "C" players. They had a number of open positions, and there was a long history of making poor hiring decisions. They really needed help! Failure to take the appropriate action resulted in several epic mis-hires over the course of a six-month period. They could not fill the positions quickly enough and had to keep several "B" and "C" players. This resulted in a number of operational shortfalls, and they found themselves having to pass up significant growth opportunities because the operation couldn't support them.

In my experience, many companies make the crucial mistake of not appreciating the role human resources managers (and the many variations for this position) play. Often, clients underestimate the complexity of human resources and the value a human resources person can bring to the organization. Many times they ask if they can just train one of their existing people for the job. This wouldn't be a problem if the hiring manager was a certified and trained human resources professional. They need a professional who already has the education (there is a certification), has the requisite experience, and can teach them what needs to be done.

In addition, professionals in the human resources field possess varying skillsets and specialties. You must fill your position with a professional who has the right ones. Many leaders either fail to fill the positions with a competent trained professional, or they fill them with someone with the wrong skillsets. In a company's early days, it needs someone who can increase the speed of recruiting, help to avoid some critical mis-hires, develop an infrastructure for onboarding and training the newly hired, and aid in building systems for accountability. Having the right person in this function can accelerate your ability to grow and scale, and it takes a tremendous amount of pressure off of the other leaders in the organization. Often, organizations fail to create and fill this position because they are concerned with the investment required to attract the right human resources person. However, you can never recover the revenue and profit that is lost by not adding that person to your infrastructure in the first place.

Another common problem area arises when the infrastructure insufficiently supports your sales and marketing strategy. We often see organizations combine sales and marketing as if they are one function. These are very different functions that require different talents and experiences. A great marketing team knows how to build a brand in the marketplace, analyze data, position a product against the competition, generate leads, and price your product correctly. Sales are about people and relationships and converting opportunities. It is rare to find someone who is great at both.

These are only two of the common structural weaknesses. There are others. For example, if you ask who is accountable for the customer voice and the customer experience across the organization, the usual answer is, "We all are." "We all are" is the same thing as "No one is." While everyone can respond to customers, someone has to define how you want everyone to respond and establish the protocols. Someone has to point out when those protocols are not being followed and when processes are broken. They need to make sure you are collecting and responding to actionable customer data too.

So when asking if you have the right structure to win, you are really trying to answer these questions: "Where are our structural weaknesses, and how are they causing our strategy to fail?"

What Percentage of the Time Are You Hiring the Right Person?

What Is Your Success Rate?

Number of People to be Replaced	Your Current Success in Hiring/ Promoting			
	25%	50%	75%	90%
10	31	17	11	10
20	67	35	24	20
40	141	72	48	40
100	357	179	120	100

Topgrading, by Bradford Smart[25]

If yours is like most companies, your hiring success rate is at best 25 percent. Hiring success means you hire a person who achieves the productivity requirements established for that position and also lives your core values. It is stunning how often a company will hire someone, realize within 90 days (the average probationary period) that they hired the wrong person, but allow that person to remain in place for years.

A poor hire is a hidden vacancy. While it appears you've filled your position, the extra management time expended and the lack of productivity (gap between the performance standard and actual performance) causes you to need more people. This is because the existing team performs less work than the same number of people performing at prescribed levels. This is exacerbated by the increased number of mistakes that occur. It creates a blind spot and an invisible profit leak. Based on the chart above, if you have a 25 percent success rate in hiring "A" players, it will take 31 hires before you acquire 10 good people. How is that for a gaping hole in your bucket? [26]

Are you currently measuring hiring success? Most companies measure employee turnover and tenure and never measure the quality of the people who were hired.

How Long Are Positions Vacant?

Do you measure the length of time a position remains open in your company? Filling a vacancy in a timely manner can become especially problematic when the job market gets tight or you create positions that require unicorns. There is an old saying: "Hire slow, and fail fast." Amend this to say, "Hire an "A" player fast."

Too often policies and organizational pressure force an organization to hire the wrong person. It becomes more important to just fill the seat than to fill the seat "right." This happens because leaders make unproductive comments that cause their team members to cut process corners, hire friends and family, and make other unwise choices that lead to bad hiring decisions. Ironically, after the dust settles, the first person to get blamed is the manager or human resources professional who tried to stop the madness to begin with.

For all the reasons discussed thus far, it ought to be clear that hiring the wrong person is a costly mistake. You are better off with an open seat than the wrong fit.

Eight Steps to Addressing Position Vacancy

- What is your strategy for finding the ideal candidate?
- How many quality candidates applied this week for each open position?
- If you are not getting enough quality candidates each week, how will you adjust your strategy?
- Does that strategy match the reality of where candidates will be found?
- Is your offer going to be attractive to your ideal candidate?
- Have you created a position that requires a unicorn?
- How competitive will you be in the marketplace?

Will using a quality recruiter increase the number of qualified candidates, improve the quality of candidates, and speed up your process? Bearing in mind that time costs money, will using a quality recruiter cost you less than continuing on your own?

These questions will help you sift through the potential candidates and make an educated hiring decision. There is no perfect equation to find the optimal candidate, but this vetting process will certainly help you succeed. Remember to review vacant positions over time to see if the company was able to perform without that position filled for a quantifiable time frame. This can help you determine if that position is integral to the success of the business, or if it can be fully eliminated so as to allot those resources elsewhere.

Is Accountability Unclear or Is Someone Accountable for Too Much?

Many organizations are held back because they fail to properly clarify accountability, responsibility, and authority in their organization. Too often we use these words interchangeably, but they are very different concepts. In most organizations there is not enough clarity around these three concepts. In his book *Scaling Up*, Verne Harnish did a great job of clarifying these points:

- ✓ **Accountability:** There must be one person in the organization who tracks progress for a function, team, division, process, customer, or project. When issues arise, this person is responsible to report those issues to the management team so that obstacles can be addressed. While this person may not have any authority and may not be a leader, they "account" for what is going on. If you designate more than one person to be accountable, then some things will fall through the cracks. You open the opportunity for confusion and finger-pointing.

✓ **Responsibility**: This falls to anyone with the "ability to respond." These are the people you want to act in some way. Ideally the people tasked with responding need to have the proper training, knowledge, experience, and time to do so well.

✓ **Authority:** This belongs to the person or team with the ability to make a decision.

Consider this great example of how this works: The CEO of a $50 million distribution company came to us because of his failing health. His company was doing well and was very profitable, but he could not figure out why he was working so hard. We asked him to provide us with his organizational chart and to define the roles of the people on the chart. For two days, one of my team members sat in his office and tracked the flow of activity. His perception of his daily routine was quite different from ours. He provided us a traditional organizational chart with his name at the top and the names of seven of his direct reports. However, his chart revealed he was really operating within a circle. He was in the center and all employees were going directly to him for everything. The CEO was accountable for everything, had all the authority, and had everyone else responding according to his orders. No wonder he was exhausted. He was a total micromanager who had not given up any accountability or authority.

We have to consider whether accountability and authority can be equal. This is a complicated question. My recommendation would be that the closer to the front line you are, more balance is encouraged. You need to empower people at the front line to have the authority to do the right things for the customer. You do not want to create bottlenecks so that customers get really upset before their complaints are resolved, particularly in this age of social media where it takes seconds for a "missile" to fly into cyberspace. Work to enable your people to handle complaints rapidly and provide them with the training, processes, and knowledge to do so. The Ritz-Carlton Hotel is a great example of this practice. They maintain a policy that empowers every front-line employee to spend up to $2,000 to resolve a customer complaint, and a manager can spend up to $5,000 to do the same.

However, as one moves up the organization we see real control getting lost. Authority does not equal control, and thus the balance between authority and accountability starts to shift. You start becoming liable for things that are well out of your control. This is why your pay grade goes up and you have to close that gap with your soft skills, education, and other abilities.[27]

Using the Gazelles Growth Tools to Help Clarify Accountability

So with all of these pain points in mind, what steps can you take to correct these issues and ensure your bucket is not leaking? Using two of the Gazelles Growth Tools, the People Accountability Chart, and The Process Accountability Chart, I challenge you to answer the following questions to close your leaks in these areas:

- What are all the roles in your company?
- Who is in charge of each role?
- What leading and lagging measures tell you that each role is functioning well? Are you measuring them?
- What are the top five to nine processes in your company?
- Who is in charge of each process?
- What leading and lagging measures tell you that each process is functioning well? Are you measuring them?
- For each position in your company have you identified each person's top five accountabilities, and how you will measure that they are met? Are you measuring them?
- How did you measure whether they were getting done?
- What key performance indicators do you use to measure high performance for each position/role/function?
- Is any one person accountable for too many key roles in the organization?
- Is there any key role or function that has no one person accountable?
- Is there any role that is not functioning well?

Do you tell people to leave early even when you are going to stay late? People tend do as you do, not as you say.

Are proper boundaries set for your employees and yourself between work and home?

Is every person challenged to finish the highest value activities first or are they filling their days with the easier lower-value tasks?

Is there a clear set of priorities to help people say "no", or is your mantra that everything is important?[28]

Key Chapter Points
Profit Leak #4: *Vacant Positions*

- You've likely invested the largest part of your budget in your people, and investing it the wrong way can create one of the biggest leaks in your bucket.

- Your focus on controlling costs may be causing you to inadvertently hinder your organization by underinvesting in people. Do you give enough consideration to how hiring the right people can bring value to and help you grow your business?

- Many organizations that grow quickly fall victim to organizational mismatch. While the positions are filled, they might as well be vacant.

- Do you have the structure best designed to serve your ideal prospects' problems better than any of your competitors? Are you set up to acquire these ideal customers?

- Each quarter evaluate your organizational structure and ask yourself how your structure may be failing to support your strategy.

- Obvious weaknesses in many companies are lack of strength in human resources, marketing, customer service, and finance.

- The average company hires an "A" player every one in four hires. If you have a 25 percent success rate in hiring "A" players, it will take 31 hires before you acquire 10 good people

- A poor hire is a hidden vacancy. Research has shown that a wrong hire can cost you up to 15 times their salary.

- Are you currently measuring hiring success? Most companies measure employee turnover and tenure and never measure the quality of the people who were hired.
- There are eight steps to addressing position vacancies.
- Know the difference between accountability, responsibility, and authority, and make clear who owns each role.
- Use the Gazelles Functional Accountability Chart and Process Accountability Chart to increase accountability clarity in your organization.

---- *Chapter 9* ----

PROFIT LEAK #5
Excessive Turnover

I n the previous chapter, we discussed the leaks caused by improperly placed team members, incorrect organizational structure, and open positions. Each of these scenarios creates enormous waste for your business. You create additional waste when you hire the wrong people for the job, mismanage, or cultivate the wrong environment for these people. That's as bad as just hiring average employees. Hiring the wrong people, mismanaging them, or creating the wrong environment can result in low turnover or excessive turnover, and both can become Leaky Buckets.

The first issue is low turnover, which often goes mostly unnoticed because it is usually considered a measure of success. Management assumes everything is great if employees are not quitting their jobs. However, on too many occasions low or no turnover is a sign of organizational complacency, weakness, or low standards. We have also seen companies with high turnover accept their turnover rate in the belief that it is common in their industry or the type of position for which they are hiring. Great companies know addressing this issue gives them a strategic advantage over their competition since turnover is a major leak in any company's bucket. The Container Store is a great example; they are experiencing 10 percent turnover in an industry where the norm is over 100 percent.[29]

Is Your Turnover Too Low?

So let's look to your own turnover and address it accordingly. No precise number can gauge whether your turnover is too low. However, if your turnover is below 10 percent, you need to take notice. You can evaluate turnover as an entire company and by function.

Some turnover is healthy, and there is always natural turnover. You might realize you made some hiring mistakes. Then again, people move, have life-changing events, career needs that may not match what you offer, and some people just need a change. Each of these occurrences is simply par for the course. By the same token, extremely low turnover is usually a sign that you are complacent, willing to accept mediocre performance, not measuring the right indicators, or don't hold people accountable for their work product.

That being said, bringing new people into your organization can have excellent benefits. The right mix of new people has a tendency to shake things up, because they breathe new life into your business. New employees come in with a desire to prove their worth. They are excited about their new position and company. They bring fresh ideas and new perspectives. They ask "why" a lot. This is a good thing. Many times an organization can get stale and then fall behind the competition. People get too comfortable with each other and the way things have always been done.

How Does Culture Affect Turnover?

If you study any organization that exemplifies sustained superior performance, you will find a remarkable culture. This culture is defined and constructed around the core values institutionalized by your executive team. In other words, the core values, when practiced on a daily basis, help top companies become more successful than their competition.

The best way to get your attention is through the eyes of a real company (we'll call it XYZ Company) that seriously underperformed against its competition. Its curse: Its performance level provided an adequate income for its main shareholder and leaders. What it did not want to address was what everyone who visited the company could see: The organization's culture could not attract or keep "A" players. Worse, its culture fostered poor performance and encouraged turnover.

XYZ Company had approximately $1 billion in sales. They were looking for someone to conduct training with their sales force, which was experiencing high turnover and had a high number of "B" and "C" players. While it would be nice for a training company to have an engagement to develop 150 salespeople, training and development was not their core issue. This company needed more sales.

The facts were alarming. The company did not have clear goals; did not fire non-performers; did not have good hiring policies; did not tie compensation to performance, etc. Finally, we asked the magic question, "What are your company's core values?"

Silence followed. The leadership had never defined and implemented core values to make this company great. What resulted were unwritten core values that were unflattering:

- <u>Mediocrity</u>: Salespeople were not working hard or trying to be their best. When selling to customers, they would give in on price because they believed they were second-rate compared to their competition. Very few salespeople proactively sought training, and when the company offered training, they did not show up.
- <u>No Accountability</u>: If people did not hit their sales targets, there were no consequences, particularly if they had been with the company for a number of years. They were just "forgiven" and still paid handsomely.
- <u>Mistrust</u>: The organization did not follow through on initiatives. They talked big and acted small. Consequently, when they said they wanted to create change, nobody took them seriously. Additionally, while the leadership indicated they had a "consumer-oriented" strategy, 80 percent of its products were "commodity-based." The company generally operated as if their strategy were "low cost."
- <u>Disrespect</u>: Senior management would begin initiatives only to have the CEO come and usurp them.

XYZ Company was growing slower and had lower margins than their competition, even though their product was just as good as others—and in some cases better. While they thought sales training would solve their problem, they were not facing the core issue: company culture. Do you think ideal performers would want to stay around this work environment? That anyone would operate at peak performance here? That with their reputation they could attract top talent?

As demonstrated above, if you do not plan your core values, they happen anyway, and the results can be devastating. The longer you wait to define and instill the right core values in your organization, the harder it will be to achieve your ideal culture and thus maximize performance.

But what does this have to do with turnover? The reality is that if you do not create a strong culture, you probably won't attract quality team members to begin with. Those who are truly "A" players will not stay with you because they will not find purpose or happiness within your business.

Are You Spending Enough Time Defining Employee Roles?

When managing employees from recruitment to retention, we place significant emphasis on defining the roles of each and every employee. I have seen firsthand how mindfully defining each employee's role, responsibilities, and success metrics creates more success on the team and within the company overall. When responsibilities are well-defined, employees feel a sense of security and safety within their jobs. They know what is to be done and how, leading to more connected team members and greater retention.

An interesting article in the *Harvard Business Review* that really drives this point home summarized a study completed by the author, Tamara Erickson, on team dynamics at the BBC and Reuters. She found that successful collaboration was better on teams when each employee's role was clearly defined. Defining individual roles impacted collaboration success more than spelling out the group's approach.

Erickson noted, "Without such clarity, team members are likely to waste energy negotiating roles or protecting turf, rather than focusing on the task."[30]

Carry this idea over into employees' everyday tasks. By clearly defining employee roles from the start, not only do we target and hire the best, most qualified candidates, but we also ensure their continued success by informing them exactly how that success will be determined and measured.

Nine Keys to Finding Your Ideal Hire

Increase your hiring, employee, and team success rate by ensuring that each position in your organization has a position description that includes:

1. Position Mission: One sentence summarizing why the position exists.
2. Job Description: Collection of tasks and responsibilities that an employee is responsible for.
3. Key Accountabilities: For what and to whom does this person have primary accountability?
4. Responsibilities: Unit of work or set of activities needed to produce some result (e.g., answering phones, writing a memo, sorting the mail, etc.).
5. Competencies: Abilities (skills) and capacity required to perform the job successfully.
6. Critical Success Factors: Provide focus on the influences that impact the performance of the job.
7. Key Process Ownership: Identify the critical processes owned by the position.
8. Key Performance Indicators: Provide visibility to performance through the use of metrics and established performance targets, thereby giving context to vague concepts.
9. Career History: The background experience typically required to have gained the level of knowledge and competency required for the position. This clarifies the outcomes they have produced in the past that would provide confidence that they will be successful in your position.

Without defining these extremely important position attributes, how would you be able to write a job advertisement? How would you know where to look for candidates? Would you really be able to truly select between job candidates with similar resumes? Of course not! The human resources team will not know what will make the ideal candidate if you do not prioritize the qualities most important about the person you want to hire. Once the person is on board, he or she will not know what they need to accomplish. As a result, they will be working hard, but with no targets in mind and little direction. The results will certainly be less than their potential.

In my experience, this is the number one failure in the hiring process. Either this step has not been performed, performed improperly, or the person hired did not match the criteria developed in the process. Often, hiring parties decide to focus on some, but not all, of the characteristics identified in the Nine Keys to Finding Your Ideal Hire and it comes back to haunt them with poor efficiency and increased turnover.

Are You as Good as You Think at Interviewing?

When I ask leaders how they learned the interview process, most tell me they learned on the job through trial and error. Most consider themselves very good at this responsibility, yet their track record proves otherwise. Prior to working with me, one client consistently chose the wrong people because "attitude" was the all-important employee trait to her. She felt that one could accomplish anything with a good attitude. As a result, her company had rampant turnover. The people who stayed were friends and family, and they were far from optimal performers. Of course, because of their relationships, it didn't matter.

To ensure your company's turnover remains as low as possible, you need a very good interviewing process. *Topgrading* by Brad Smart includes an interview process that boasts a 90 percent success rate in hiring an "A" player for any position in your company. Even then, you have to be disciplined in your hiring practices. The *Topgrading* process can fail for those who are inconsistent and do not follow all the procedural steps.[31]

Another issue that arises: Some people should not be interviewing job candidates to begin with. For example, some interviewers spend more time talking than the actual interviewee. They can't help themselves. They are always selling. They overconfidently believe they only need 10 minutes to spot talent. What candidate can't fake it for 10 minutes? If someone is not usually a good listener or has a bad track record after being properly trained in the *Topgrading* interview process, they should be excluded from the main process, regardless of title. If they need to be in the process because of title, leave them for the end of the process, after the talented interviewers are comfortable that they have a good candidate. Then you can let the salespeople close the deal.

There has been much written on interviewing and selecting talent. As I speak with clients—even those who use some of the best interviewing techniques—our talks reveal they often miss the main point. Finding the ideal person for each position requires understanding what constitutes "talent" for that position. The people tasked with filling a position need to ask themselves, "What talents are required to perform this job very well?" That is the key question.

When filling a job, interviewers often look for:

1. Education
2. Experience in the role
3. Experience in the industry
4. Personality
5. Aptitude

While these are important considerations, if the applicant lacks the core talents specific to the position, he/she can possess all of the above and still not perform the way you want. For example, if you want to hire a head of strategic planning for a large company, you should consider a person whose talents include the ability to:

1. Ask questions that most others do not think to ask.
2. See patterns in data that most others cannot see.
3. Persuade others who want to continue with the status quo to consider alternative possibilities.
4. Present information in a way that others can't.
5. Ask very difficult questions of people who are their organizational superiors.
6. Have the self-confidence to go against the grain and not be "yes men."

The applicants may have experience in strategic planning, have worked in your industry, have great personalities, and be really smart. The problem is that interviewers typically do not even identify the other key talents as necessary, let alone probe for and get a sense they exist in the applicants. Ironically, if someone has more of the latter and is light on the former, they will outperform the people who have more of the former on their resume.

How Robust Is Your Onboarding Process?

If you bring your new employees on board in the wrong fashion, you may permanently destroy your relationship with them. Many new employees leave within their first six months.[32] Failure to bring them on properly in the first place is at the root of this problem. Organizations with strong onboarding processes save themselves a lot of time and money. In addition, they usually need fewer employees because the people they have are top performers.

It has been found that the companies that participated in coaching programs (typically lasting from six months to one year) reported six times the return value on their bottom line.[33] In addition, the companies that provided coaching programs to their management and leadership teams realized improvements in productivity, quality, organizational strength, customer service, and shareholder value. They also received fewer customer complaints and were more likely to retain individuals who received coaching. Individuals who received coaching reported experiencing better relationships with their direct reports, immediate supervisors, peers, and clients. They also reported better teamwork and job satisfaction, reduced conflict, and renewed organizational commitment. Organized training and ongoing coaching is essential in the first 90 days of employment and beyond to ensure you are capable of retaining the talent you acquire.[34]

What Actions Can Be Taken?

Shift to a game plan to actually hire strong talent and retain them. Hire the wrong people and you will find yourself hiring again. Hire the wrong people and choose not to invest time and energy into their development and, once again, you'll be hiring again. To avoid the pitfalls, take tried and true steps to ensure you are putting a strong plan in place to hire the best team for you and your company:

- **Core Values.** Create and institutionalize your core values. Finding your core values does not need to be a long exercise. A good facilitator can work with your senior management team and identify and define core values within one to four hours, depending on the size of the group. It can be fun. On a more serious note, determining your core values is critical to really understanding what drives your company's vision.
- **Be Clear.** Answer the following questions for every role in your company:
  1. Are expectations clear?
  2. Are expectations realistic?
  3. Is management sending mixed messages?
  4. Does the person have the tools to do their job well?
  5. Is the organization creating any barriers preventing them from doing their job well?
- **Profile Regularly.** Implement a position-profiling process into your company. The process must answer these questions before beginning your recruiting process. Make sure everyone involved in the selection process knows the answers to these questions, and measure your hiring decisions against how well the candidates match the criteria. For those of you reading this and saying that you'll take attitude over credentials any day, you'd better get both. Ask questions like:
  1. What is the title of the position?
  2. What is the brief description of the position? In other words, what would not happen in this company if this position did not exist?
  3. What are the three to five most important measurable and specific goals or objectives this person will be held accountable to achieve?
  4. Who are the customers/clients this position serves, and how do these customers/clients measure service?
  5. What key processes does this position own, and how do you measure that the process is working properly?

6. What other key/critical processes are associated with the position, and how do you measure that the person in this position is doing their part well?

7. Does the position have any certification and/or licensing requirements, and has the applicant met them?

8. What is the position responsible for, and what is it accountable for?

9. What talents must this person have to be successful?

10. How are you going to verify these talents in the interview process?

11. Who has input in this person's performance review, determines their compensation/raises, and is responsible to help them develop?

12. What do you see as the biggest challenges to success in this position, and what steps must be taken to address them?

13. What are the minimum qualifications for the position in terms of education, functional experience, and industry experience?

14. What specific industry knowledge does this person need to have?

15. What capabilities must the applicant be proficient in or excel at to be successful?

16. What would you say are the critical obstacles for those filling the position, and what are the steps that must be taken to address them.

17. Describe the ideal person for this position in terms of how they address new decisions/challenges, interact with people, deal with pace in the environment, and approach rules and procedures.

18. How many subordinates does the position have? Describe the relationship this position has with its subordinates (e.g., can they hire and fire people?).

- **Create an Onboarding Program.** A 90-day onboarding program is an imperative for every single new employee. A complete program includes:
  1. Traditional orientation
  2. Immersion of the new employee into the organizational culture
  3. Detailed performance plan for the initial 90 days
  4. Scheduled ongoing interactions (daily and weekly) with their manager(s) to assure/enable efficient ramp-up

5. Scheduled training on all aspects of the processes, procedures, technology, company, vendors, products, services, and industry necessary to do the job well

6. Scheduled interaction with various parts of the organization

Each of these actions provide opportunities to become a better leader and assist in getting, keeping, and growing a strong team. As you hone these skills, you'll find you position employees for extensive success throughout their time with your company.

Key Chapter Points
Profit Leak #5: *Excessive Turnover*

- Do not accept high turnover even if it is common in your industry for a particular position.
- Low turnover (usually below 10 percent) shows you are complacent, willing to accept mediocre performance, not measuring the right indicators, or don't hold people accountable for their work product.
- New employees come in with a desire to prove their worth. They are excited about their new position and company and they bring fresh ideas and new perspectives.
- Your culture has a direct impact on turnover. A poor culture turns over "A" players faster. If you do not create a strong culture, you probably won't attract quality team members to begin with.
- Failure to define positions well is the number one reason for hiring mistakes.
- When responsibilities are well-defined, employees feel a sense of security and safety within their jobs.
- Use the nine keys to the ideal hire identified in this chapter.
- Read Brad Smart's *Topgrading* and use the interview process in the book. It boasts a 90 percent success rate in hiring the right person.
- If the applicant lacks the core talents specific to the position, he/she can possess your educational experience, role experience, industry

experience, culture, and aptitude requirements and will still fail in the role.

- If you bring your new employees on board in the wrong fashion, you may permanently destroy your relationship with them.
- Companies that provided coaching to their leadership and management teams reported they received six times the value to their bottom line.

PART III
STRATEGY LEAKS

"However beautiful the strategy, you should occasionally look at the results."
—**Unknown**[35]

Chapter 10

PROFIT LEAK #6
Action Without Purpose

U p to this point, we have discussed the types of leaks caused by waste your team created. Hiring the wrong people, providing insufficient training, and not creating a bountiful and healthy culture for those you lead can all create enormous leaks in your bucket. Even if you have the right people with the right attitude in the right place, you are not exempted from the responsibility of providing them with the strategy to succeed in the game of business. Strategy is an important component for any thriving business. If the people are the "who" in your company, the strategy is the "why" and the "what." It is the direction you give them and the new rules by which your team will play the game.[36]

Why Purpose Matters

Place "purpose" at the forefront of any new business. As you develop and grow, ensure you maintain that vision and mission through thick and thin. This is a critical issue that often fails to get enough attention. Many a profit leak can be connected to a business that has lost its purpose, or even worse, never had one from the start. Purpose is like a lantern in a dark cave, guiding you through the unknown and helping you safely reach your destination.

Many business owners mistakenly believe their purpose is to make money or create financial gain. Maybe you're thinking, *Isn't that the purpose of being in a for-profit business?* Certainly, that may be one of your goals, but I can confidently tell you that making money is not aligned with a proper and meaningful purpose. By serving a business purpose well and doing it in a profitable manner, you will make money. Remember, the more important your overall purpose, the better you can serve your community at large, and inevitably, the more money you can ultimately make by striving to fulfill it.

If I met you at a party and asked you to tell me about your business, where would you start? Most people default to discussing their role, title, function, product, or service they offer. For example, one person might tell me they are the managing partner in an accounting firm, or a tax accountant, or an auditor. A CEO might tell me he owns a company that manufactures retail skincare products. However, no matter how hard they sell it, those are merely titles, and roles, not purpose. If you look at the marketplace, there is an oversupply of just about every product and service you can name. Think about it. When was the last time you thought, "There isn't a tax accountant, lawyer, or banker to be found anywhere?" When was the last time you heard someone say, "I wish I had more choices of toothpaste, chips, haircare, coffee, or skincare products because there are just not enough of them?" It just isn't going to happen. There is an oversupply of products and services, and they are available everywhere you go, as well as online and over the phone, and can be delivered twenty-four hours a day, seven days a week.

Now imagine if those same people had a different view of their purpose. As an example, let's look at an accounting firm focused on increasing the wealth of its clients. This firm builds a set of practice areas in tax, audit, technology, wealth management, etc. They create a team for each client that uses the strengths of each team member to devise the best annual strategy to help maximize their client's wealth. While you may point out that every sizeable firm has the same practice areas, this firm's view of what they are doing and why they exist is the difference-maker for their business. It should cause them to forge a nontraditional client relationship structure. To achieve their purpose, they must build specialized tool kits, focus on unique resources, and treat their clients with very specific intention. Not every accounting firm is creating the kind of relationship with their clients that would allow for such positive outcomes to occur, thereby leaving valuable opportunity on the table.

Establishing your purpose allows you to address the following important questions:

1. What is the primary difference you want your organization to make for your community of clients?
2. How is the community being served, and what would be lost without your organization?
3. What will your client relationships and experience need to resemble?
4. What boundaries and rules must you learn to break?
5. Why will the best employees want to work for you rather than your competition?

The answers to these questions will unlock doors that would otherwise remain closed and doors that lead you to the cusp of great opportunity. By defining these answers, you can begin to recognize great results you never thought possible.

What Does It Mean to Act with Purpose?

Your purpose can be bold and transformative to solve the world's biggest problems. If you are one of these leaders, you may launch impactful organizations such as City Year, Tesla, and SKS Microfinance. The underlying purposes of these companies are really exciting because they all encompass a mission to change the world in some way. For some companies, purpose means changing an industry or solving a problem. Airbnb.com, Amazon, Google, PayPal, and Facebook are all great examples of this. However, you may look at these examples and think your own company could never be as exciting as these, but you can still make a difference. You must find your purpose. Purpose ensures that most anything of consequence occurs, compels you and others to excel, gives work more meaning, and brings people together to serve others at extraordinary levels.

Have you ever noticed that when you act with purpose, you act with more energy and enthusiasm? You are probably willing to give more effort to something that really matters to you! Compare that energy and effort to something that may be important but does not pull at your heartstrings. Worse, consider what your commitment is to an endeavor that has not captured your mind or heart. You will just go through the motions. Too often I find that most employees are not engaged because they lack this crucial investment. It would be safe to say their leaders have failed to instill purpose.

You know you are acting with purpose when your work is not about the revenue or the profit. It is much greater than that. The purpose does not change but inspires it. It is compelling enough that it gets people to work around obstacles. They expect those obstacles and only see them as challenges to be conquered. When the purpose is important to someone, they are inspired to volunteer for extra work. They volunteer to take on challenges and to solve problems.

U.S. Andersen said, "The great men of this world accomplish in an hour what other mortals accomplish in a year. Yet they are not more active. Their activity is guided, powerful, sure, because they are directed to their objectives by the unlimited resources and power of the Universal Subconscious Mind."[37] Anyone can hire employees and get minimum performance out of them. But purposeful action is monumental. Great success is achievable when you create an army of employees who believe in your goals and aspire to do whatever it takes to reach them.

How Do You Find Your Purpose?

Most times leaders feel as if they are trapped in a box. That box revolves around products and services and does not consider the problems and challenges of people they want to serve. By understanding purpose, you can move with the changing needs of your customers and evolve your products and services. Too often business leaders try to force the external world to buy what they want to sell. They fail to consider whether what they want to sell is a real need and if there is already too much supply that solves that need. If the need is already well-served or overserved, pumping more supply into the market without addressing a new critical purpose to the buyer will surely result in a painful journey for you and your colleagues. The best purposes are those that identify and then solve pending needs.

Understanding how to discover purpose is an integral piece to any organization. To aid you in that discovery, I offer you five categories of purposeful movement for your business. Purposeful companies usually try to do more than one of these. Great companies must *accomplish*, at minimum, one:

1. **Disrupting Your Industry.** Airbnb changed the lodging industry forever. They created a very cost-effective and easy way for anyone to list their space and book unique accommodations anywhere in the world. By doing so, they made traveling more affordable and accessible for many people.

2. **Uncommon Services.** Provide service at a level that goes beyond your competition in a way that is essential to your target customer. The traditional companies that come to mind are Ritz-Carlton and Nordstrom. However, in a less traditional sense I think of Amazon, where you can purchase almost anything twenty-four/seven. They offer these products at prices that are usually below MSRP and, in many cases, deliver them to your doorstep on the same day you order them, and all done with a few keystrokes.

3. **Change the World.** Purposeful organizations change the world. I am a proud board member and Red Jacket Society member at City Year, where we believe education can empower every child to reach his or her potential. We recognize that children in high-poverty communities have external obstacles that can interfere with their ability to get to school and be ready and able to learn. City Year helps with these challenges. Our purpose is to change the world by providing a strong education one student at a time.

4. **Excellence.** You can always find ways to change the features of products by increasing their speed, beauty, functionality, and many other qualities.

No company is going to get it right with every product, but Apple, Samsung, Ikea, Dyson, and 3M have produced products that have really stood out from their competitors in specific categories and could be considered excellent.

5. **Information and Communication.** Technology has caused this category of purpose to explode over the last 10 years. You can't have this conversation without Google, but you also have to consider Facebook, WeChat, WhatsApp, Slack, and the myriad of additional tools that allow people to share information, find people and things, exchange knowledge, discover, and communicate.

Look at purpose through these five lenses and determine which of the five you are really passionate about. Then address, "What purpose can my company serve within that category" to ensure you are choosing a purpose that is not being served to the level you believe it could or should be. The key is to think big! Consider your purpose to be a pursuit rather than a destination. It will be a mantra that you and your organization will need to constantly improve and perfect.

Purpose Leads to Differentiated Operations

Once you have outlined a great purpose, you will find that it leaves you with many options in how you can serve the marketplace. Until you settle on the need you want to solve, you really do not have a proper lens for products and services to offer. Choosing to bypass these five categories of purpose will eventually lead to cloudy vision and poor performance among your team members. Inevitably, it leads to waste. Identifying and eliminating that waste will allow you to be a lot more profitable than the competition. You can also use that extra cash flow to fund what is more important to a customer.

Southwest Airlines provides a great example of a company that identified waste in their industry. There has been much written about Southwest, including the book *Nuts* by Kevin and Jackie Freiberg. Herb Kelleher, CEO of Southwest, played his part in helping reinvent air travel. Kelleher's purpose was to "enable people who catch the bus to fly." To do that, he knew the cost structure of the traditional airline had to change. It meant his company would "stop doing" the things his competitors did not understand were unnecessary. He sought to prevent waste, defined as the costs incurred that did not add value to the customer he was trying to serve. Examples of the key choices Kelleher made:

- You can only make reservations on the Southwest Airlines website.
- Onboard amenities are limited.
- Planes fly to fewer than 100 airports, avoiding those with high gate fees, even though these airports might be less convenient for travelers.
- The fleet is limited to only one airplane model (the 737).

These choices have resulted in Southwest Airlines being profitable every year since its inception. In a period when all other major airlines went bankrupt and many had to consolidate to survive. If you look at the choices Southwest made during that time, you'll quickly recognize that their elimination of waste and focus on a singular purpose positioned them to succeed.[38]

Six Ways to Bring Purpose to Life in Your Organization

So what actions can you and your business take to home in on your greatest purpose? Start with these:

1. Define your purpose.
2. Include your "story" as part of your orientation process. If possible, have the CEO or another senior leader tell the story to new hires.
3. Regularly reinforce your purpose in everything you do, and make sure your company decisions are tied to your purpose.
4. Get out of your office to start talking to existing and potential customers, and make sure you know what is important to them.
5. Develop measures to make sure that everyone in your company knows what it will take to continually move closer to your purpose.
6. At your annual planning session ask questions like, "How can we better serve our purpose?"

Key Chapter Points
Profit Leak #6: *Action Without Purpose*

- The more important your overall purpose, the better you can serve your community at large, and the more money you can ultimately make by striving to fulfill it.
- Purpose is never about revenue and profit. Purpose is not about products and services. It is about problems and challenges of people you want to serve.
- Having your employees act with purpose will inspire change.
- When you act with purpose, you act with more energy and enthusiasm.
- When the purpose is important to someone they are inspired to volunteer for extra work. They volunteer to take on challenges and to solve problems.
- Establishing your purpose allows you to address the following important questions:
- What is the primary difference you want your organization to make for your community of clients?
- How is the community being served, and what would be lost without your organization?
- What will your client relationships and experience need to resemble?
- What boundaries and rules must you learn to break?
- Why will the best employees want to work for you rather than your competition?
- Purpose usually drives your organization to accomplish one of the following: disrupt your industry, provide uncommon services, change the world, cause excellence, or explode information and communication.
- Purpose leads to differentiated operations.
- By understanding purpose, you can move with the changing needs of your customers and evolve your products and services.
- We identified six ways to bring purpose to life in your organization.

―――――――・ *Chapter 11* ・―――――――

PROFIT LEAK #7
Failing to Differentiate Properly

Albert Einstein said, "We can't solve problems using the same kind of thinking we used when we created them."[39] Action without purpose is like walking through a dark house trying to find the doorway out. You simply walk in circles, spinning your wheels but recognizing no real productivity. So once we decide on purposeful action, we then have to figure out how our decisions and behaviors are unique. We all want to stand out, in a good way. Sounding like everyone else is almost as bad as not being heard at all.

We all have an idealized image of our company and ourselves. Even when we look in the mirror, our preconceived notions cloud the image that is staring right back at us. We then look around at the competition and think, with a chuckle, that they are their own worst enemies. It is so easy for us to see our own business with pride, even when glaring problems exist. After all, you know the obstacles you have overcome to get to this point. Most experts will tell you that maintaining an inaccurate perception of your real self can cause enormous profit leaks, mostly because you are blinded by your own pride or misconceptions. In other words, you don't even know what you don't even know. This issue relates to the growth in the size of your bucket, which usually could be much larger because of the many customers who were won and then lost and the ones never gained.

Have you wondered why your customer retention rate is not higher? Or is customer retention good, but new business generation trends are below expectations? Have you yet to figure out how to have a larger share of ideal customers? These issues may be indications that you're not able to see the true you in the mirror! I often listen to CEOs and their leadership teams talk about their companies in ways that defy the facts. It is great to be proud. It's important to be positive, and having the right attitude is critical. However, your real problems begin when you are not willing to face the brutal facts.

When new clients are not easily acquired, it may not be a problem with the industry or the prospects. The problem usually resides within your company. The marketplace is telling you that even if you are different from your competitors, the differences in your products and services are not compelling enough; your marketing and sales efforts and materials sound like everyone else's; breaks in your sales and marketing processes are going unchecked; or your sales and marketing are not reality, and they see the real you. If you do not address these issues, the prospective buyers will continue to believe you are just like everyone else and will see no compelling reason to use you to solve their needs and problems. Frankly, many buyers use the company that is closest, most convenient, least expensive, or use some other nonsensical or illogical reason to pick a vendor, product, or service. When you look into most industries, lots of opportunities exist to be different and gobble share of the market, even if the market itself is not growing.

If customer retention should be higher, it is not because customers are disloyal and the product or service you're offering is inferior. You may want to consider three potential causes:

1. The person you have made responsible for overseeing the processes for customer retention is not the right person (or you don't have one);
2. The unique attributes of your products or services are not compelling enough for them to stay; or

3. You have the wrong team, and the mistakes they are making are causing you to lose clients.

Too often companies are so focused on new business that they have not calculated how much their customer retention leak is costing them. Consider the three issues above and, at a minimum, establish key performance indicators that alert you to leaks in your bucket. Once you have identified, captured, and optimized the right key performance indicators, they can be used in marketing to acquire new customers.

Are You Differentiating Yourself from the Competition?

In most industries it is more and more challenging to be unique. It is much more realistic and achievable to be unusual. In reality, someone has to be the perceived industry leader. Does your business have an unusual offering that differentiates your products and services from those offered by your competition? For example, these search engine(s): Google, Bing, Yahoo, Ask, AOL, and WOW were the top six as of September 1, 2016. However, Google's unique monthly visitors were 1.61 million, a number equal to the other five combined.[40]

So how has Google differentiated their service from others? The many reasons include:

1. **Speed!** Everyone knows that in search engines, the name of the game is speed, and no one has been able to do it better than Google.
2. **Talent!** They would not be able to stay ahead of the speed game without having an amazing culture of the hardest working, most competitive, and smartest talent on the planet. They put an awful lot of effort into keeping it that way.
3. **Branding!** According to Forbes magazine they have the second most powerful brand on the planet, only behind Apple.[41] Not too shabby! They may be on the path to becoming the number one brand on Earth. In a 2013 study by SurveyMonkey examining

CEO assumptions, respondents were given two search result pages, one with a page header labeled "Google" and the other with a page header labeled "Bing," and asked which page of results they preferred. Even when they merely swapped the page header labels, more users preferred the Google search results. There is no coincidence in that decision—the brand is perceived to be that much more unique and unusual than the competition.[42]

Are You Guilty of Working on Intuition versus Knowledge?

There are a lot of ways to add value to your product or service to distinguish your company from your competitors. Creating your unusual value proposition takes creativity and a true understanding of the needs, wants, and desires of your target client. Too often leaders are working on intuition rather than knowledge when attempting to create their offerings. This practice severely hampers the growth of their businesses.

A good example is a business services company with which I have worked. They have had a long history of high customer retention. They know this retention has to do with doing something right, and that "something" does not allow competitors to steal their customers. However, they had been unable to define that "something" in order to use it to help them get new business. While the CEO was certain it was their service, they could not articulate the specifics in their sales and marketing efforts. I know this for two reasons. The first is that the company was operating on an "everything is equally important" mentality in their approach to service. After conducting a confidential customer feedback study, they learned there were some very specific factors that made them different and were essential to their success. Second, the company had failed repeatedly to increase its market share. No matter what they believed, the market was speaking to them by their buying behaviors!

The key to gaining knowledge lies outside of your building. Your salespeople do not have the answers you think they have. Your executive team must use a third party for assistance or visit and call customers and prospects themselves. After speaking to many business owners over the years, it is clear to me that most businesses have little understanding of what is truly important to their customers and have a limited understanding of the competitive landscape. They gather little or no external data and operate on false assumptions. As a result, their failure to differentiate themselves from competitors is inevitable. While everyone needs to address basic factors like price, quality, and timeliness, high-growth companies gather external data to help validate and identify what really matters to their target customers.

What Elements Constitute an Unusual Offering?

To help your business grow, let's talk about the notion of creating an unusual offering. In reality, your unusual offering may not need to be a dramatic change from your current offering. You may already have an unusual offering that you have not yet isolated. You want a good bundle or aggregation of products and services that helps solve customers' needs in a special way, while totally fitting their situation. You may have the same mix of elements as your competition, but you can combine them differently or decide to add or subtract items from your offering in untraditional ways. You must also consider your potential customers' options when configuring your bundle. Depending on your core client and the options available to them, you need to consider how the following elements add value to your unusual offering:

- **Price.** What is their total cost today? Do they know what their total cost is? What would additional features, benefits, and services be worth to your prospect in terms of time, value to their customers, the growth of their business, reducing their stress, etc.? If you added new features, services, and benefits would you increase prices, or would you just be increasing your cost of doing business? A client of mine in the benefits insurance industry does an excellent job of this. Too often companies focus too much just on what their insurance premiums are going to be. However, this client helps companies manage and reduce the total cost of offering employee benefits. They spend significant time educating clients on understanding how the system works, how employees influence cost, how to help reduce employee absenteeism, and how wellness programs can improve employee retention and engagement.

- **Cost/Risk Reduction.** How can you modify your offering in a way that can substantially reduce customer costs? How can the design of your product or service reduce risk for your customer? Many companies give thirty-day free trials and money back guarantees as inducements to allow customers a chance to experience their product or service. Obviously you should not make such an offering without being able to back up your promises. The risk you are removing should be tied to the main reason someone would want to try your service in the first place.

- **Trends.** What trends are occurring technologically, economically, and environmentally industry-wide that call for a new advancement in how your product or service is sold, delivered, distributed, or marketed? Skype took advantage of the facts that their target customers had and would have a good internet service and that long-distance calling was ridiculously expensive. They were able to provide Voice Over Internet Protocol (VOIP) without needing the infrastructure of a telephone company. Customers needed no handsets and could use tools and technology already available to them. By making Skype accessible to the average person, they stole significant share from the traditional telecoms.[43]

- **Performance.** What performance enhancement to your product or service is the most valuable to your customer? Would your customer pay more for this enhancement, and would you lose customers to a competitor that made the enhancement while you did not? Is this enhancement necessary to keep up with minimum expectations? At what point does the performance improvement no longer make a difference in the customer's buying patterns? Many times people think this is only a product issue. However, I find it is critical in business services. For example, many marketing firms have failed in recent years to meet the needs of their customers. As we all know, the world of marketing has changed dramatically. Interactive and social media has been a critical landscape that everyone is still exploring and learning.

Business owners need marketing to build, nurture, and preserve their brand to ultimately support their growth requirements. The outcomes they believe they have been receiving from interactive firms have not met their expectations. The firms that have delivered have been rewarded handsomely.

- **Customization.** To what extent does customization to product or service significantly enhance value? Many of my customers offer different bundles of their products and/or services to change the perceived value to a customer. A simple example of this is how Activate Group Inc. bundles services to drive better outcomes for clients. We do this through Bronze, Silver, Gold, and Platinum business coaching programs. I can assure you that our Gold and Platinum subscribers experience better and faster outcomes than the Bronze customers.

- **Design.** To what extent does design make a difference in the usability of your product or service? Can design make your product more appealing or usable? Technology and people intensity are the two key levers here. Some businesses guarantee you will always talk to a human being. In others, you will never talk to one. How do you use technology to increase speed of a critical aspect of the product or service, added convenience, functionality, integration, accuracy, consistency, etc.?

- **Brand/Status.** To what extent does brand or status influence the buyer? The internet has allowed some companies to rise to the top and get national and international recognition for a fraction of the cost that was once required. Dollar Shave Club recently was purchased for $1 billion by Unilever. Founded in 2011, this company used YouTube videos to acquire 3.2 million members and was on track to reach $200 million in revenue in 2016.[44]

- **Accessible.** How can you make your offering more accessible to your target client? What channels do you use to access clients? Netflix stole significant market share from Blockbuster and even cable companies when they determined that customers preferred streaming video over DVDs.[45]

Evaluating and then answering each of these questions will help you not only realize but truly define what your unusual offering is or will be. It is also important to note that you have to make a choice. Too many leaders take the position that they will offer the lowest price, best service, and highest quality. That is a business model that is guaranteed to fail. At best, you can focus on two out of the three but only really be best at one. You will need to choose. As mentioned above, you likely already have some of the framework in place and just need to identify what truly makes your company special and how you can differentiate yourself from the competition.

This Is Not a Marketing Program!

Have you confused having an unusual offering with changing your marketing materials? Many owners create their marketing before they really develop an unusual offering. Worse, some develop an unusual offering on paper that they cannot back up through operations. It should work in reverse. Once you develop and master your unusual offering, customers will easily agree to choose you over your competition. Then you can create marketing campaigns that make it easy for people to notice you and have salespeople who can convert the core customers as they walk into the sales process.

Seven Ways to Be a True Differentiator

Steps can be taken to ensure you are not leaking unnecessary profits by lacking an unusual offering and demonstrating to your market you are a true differentiator. To start:

1. <u>Communicate</u> - Get out of your office and start talking to existing and potential customers. Too often companies believe they already know what customers want. Typically, they are wrong. How do I know? The same companies that tell me they have it figured out are also having difficulty acquiring new customers.

2. <u>Focus on Change</u> - Once those difference-makers have been identified, you must focus on improving internal processes to become the best in

the industry at delivering those differences. In other words, there is a strategy in theory but not in practice.

3. <u>Be Accountable</u> - Third, leaders fail to measure whether they are delivering an unusual level of performance on the difference-makers. As a result, there is little accountability for delivering on your strategy.

4. <u>Create Infrastructure</u> - Have a process to help your current customers recognize the value they are receiving

5. <u>Shine Bright</u> - Capture and market your key distinguishing factors effectively.

6. <u>Prove It</u> - Provide the evidence to your sales force to show prospects what makes you unusual. Make sure this is part of the sales process.

7. <u>Request Feedback</u> - Gather regular feedback from the people who choose not to buy from you and even those who leave you after becoming customers.

In all likelihood, each of these areas is causing you to leak generous profits from your bucket and perhaps to your competition. If you identify the leaks quickly and begin plugging the holes, you'll rapidly eliminate the waste.

Become a Differentiator

Creating differentiation isn't always easy, and many times it is good to use an outside facilitator to help you through the process. A number of tools can help you work through differentiation. Consider for example:

Four Actions Framework

In *Blue Ocean Strategy*, authors W. Chan Kim and Renée Mauborgne offer the "Four Actions Framework" whereby leaders are challenged to consider the buyer value elements and to craft a new value curve. They suggest four key questions to ask to challenge an industry's strategic logic and business model to help you differentiate:

1. Reduce: Which factors should be reduced well below the industry's standards?

2. Eliminate: Which factors does the industry take for granted that should be eliminated?

3. Create: Which factors should be created that the industry has never offered?

4. Raise: Which factors should be raised well above the industry standards?

In a famous example, Kim and Mauborgne referred to Yellow Tail Wines. They approached the wine industry differently from the premium and budget wine segments to create their own segment. If you are a wine connoisseur you know that the wine industry had long competed on tannins, oak, complexity, and aging to differentiate themselves. Yellow Tail Wine steered away from the appreciation of fine grapes and historic wine craftsmanship to gain a foothold in the market. They believed the average consumer found choosing wine overwhelming and intimidating. Yellow Tail changed this by creating ease of selection. They reduced the range of wines offered by only having two selections—Chardonnay and Shiraz—while removing all the unnecessary technical jargon. They made purchasing wine fun and adventurous with their labeling and marketing and created an "easy drinking" category.[46]

Business Model Canvas

In the *Business Model Generation,* Alexander Osterwalder and Yves Pigneur used "The Business Model Canvas" to help you work through the nine business model building blocks that form the basis for your business. The canvas is a tool designed to help you look at the nine elements of a business model and to make significant choices that will make your business model uniquely different and preferable from your competition.

1. Customer Segments. This building block describes the different groups of people or organizations an enterprise aims to reach and service. They are separated based on common needs, behaviors, and other attributes so they can be better served.
    *   Do they deserve a distinct offer?
    *   Are they reached through different channels?

- Do they require different types of relationships?
- Do they have substantially different profitability?
- Is there a willingness to pay for different aspects of the offer?

2. Value Propositions. This building block describes the bundle of products and services to solve customers' problems or needs in an unusual way. You have to decide on what is most important to them and how they are underserved:

- Newness
- Getting the job done
- Price
- Accessibility
- Performance
- Design
- Cost reduction
- Convenience
- Customization
- Brand status
- Risk reduction
- Usability

3. Channels. This building block describes how a company communicates with and reaches its customer segments to deliver a value proposition.

- How you communicate with and reach your customer.
- How do they want to be reached versus how you are reaching them?
- How are channels being integrated?
- Which work best?
- Which are cost efficient?
- How do you integrate with your customer routines?

4. Key Activities. This building block describes the most important things a company must to do to make its business model work.

- Production problem-solving
- Platform/network
- What are the three to five processes in your business that would cause your company to mushroom exponentially if you were better,

faster, and/or cheaper than everyone else? Who is that one person who owns each process? How are you measuring that you are best in the world?

5. Customer Relationships. This building block describes the types of relationships a company establishes with specific customer segments.
   - What is the right mix of people versus automated relationship?
   - Customer acquisitions
   - Customer retention
   - Upselling
   - What does the customer expect?
   - What does each decision cost?
   - How are relationships integrated with the rest of the business model?
   - Personal assistance
   - Dedicated personal assistance
   - Self-service
   - Automated service
   - Communities
   - Co-creative

6. Revenue Streams. This building block represents the cash a company generates from each customer segment.
   - What are your pricing mechanism options? Fixed, bargaining, auction, volume, yield?
   - Revenue streams? Free, asset sales, subscription, advertising, usage, licensing, brokerage, leasing, renting, lending, product sales?

7. Key Resources. This building block describes the most important assets required to make a business model work.
   - Financial, physical, intellectual, human, owned, leased, or acquired from partners.
   - Which ones should you own because they constitute your competitive advantage and will be what makes you different?
   - Which ones will be needed that are essential to your differentiation strategy?

8. Key Partnerships. This building block describes the network of suppliers and partners who make the business model work.
   - Strategic alliances between non-competitors
   - Strategic alliance with competitors
   - Joint ventures to develop a new business
   - Buyer-supplier relationships to assure reliable supply
9. Cost Structure. This building block describes the most important costs incurred while operating under a particular business model.
   - Direct materials that will be required for each sale.
   - Direct labor cost that will be required for each sale.
   - Cost to acquire each customer?
   - Marketing costs to create brand awareness?
   - Administrative costs to manage the company (management, support people, phones, facility, technology, etc.)
   - Cost of the infrastructure to service and support the customer (technology and people, etc.)[47]

Key Chapter Points
Profit Leak #7: *Failing to Differentiate Properly*

- Maintaining an inaccurate perception of your real self can cause enormous profit leaks, mostly because you are blinded by your own pride or misconceptions.
- If customer retention should be higher, customer disloyalty and/or inferior products or services may not be the issues. You may want to consider three potential causes:
  1. The person you have made responsible for overseeing the processes for customer retention is not the right person (or you don't have one);
  2. The unique attributes of your products or services are not compelling enough for them to stay; or
  3. You have the wrong team, and the mistakes they are making are causing you to lose clients.

- Once you have captured and optimized the right key performance indicators for keeping the right customers they can be used in marketing to acquire new customers.
- When new clients are not easily acquired, it may not be a problem with the industry or the prospects.
  - The problem usually resides within your company.
  - The marketplace is telling you that even if you are different from your competitors, the differences in your products and services are not compelling enough; your marketing and sales efforts and materials sound like everyone else's; breaks in your sales and marketing processes are going unchecked; or your sales and marketing are not reality and they see the real you.
- Make sure you are using knowledge rather than intuition when selecting the core differentiators.
  - You have to get out of your office on a regular basis to talk to existing and potential customers.
  - Do not leave it to your sales team!
- You can create an unusual offering through price, cost/risk reduction, addressing the trends, performance, customization, design, brand/status, and accessibility.
- Too many leaders take the position they will offer the lowest price, best service, and highest quality.
  - At best you can focus on two out of three but will only really be best at one.
- Unusual offering is not a marketing program.
  - Your marketing program articulates the most important specific aspects of your unusual offering that will cause people to choose you over your competition.
- Once difference-makers have been identified, you must focus on improving internal processes to become the best in the industry at delivering those differences.
- You must measure that you are delivering on your difference-makers.
- We identified six ways to be a true differentiator.

- Use the "Four Actions Framework" and consider the buyer value elements and craft a new value curve.
- Use "The Business Model Canvas" to work through the nine business model building blocks that form the basis for your business. Compare your choices to those of your key competitors to check for real meaningful differences for your customer.

———┤ *Chapter 12* ├———

PROFIT LEAK #8
Focusing on Tactics Instead of Strategy

D o you feel like you are different from the competition? The previous chapter should help you consider this extraordinarily important question. Part of the way leaders and their companies stand above the rest is through shifting from tactics to a well-conceptualized strategy. Many people use the words "tactics" and "strategies" almost interchangeably. This is a grave mistake as they are two very different concepts. In fact, confusing one for the other is not just a misconception, it can actually lead to profit leaks. The truth is that tactics and strategy are complementary concepts, working together to accomplish goals.

The best way to look at the difference between the two is to understand that strategy defines your ultimate destination or goals for the long term (vision), identifies your risks, isolates the challenges and obstacles to success, and determines your key success factors. Tactics are the specific actions you'll take to accomplish your strategy. For example, Uber strategized to simplify arranging a ride. The strategy was to use technology to connect people who had vehicles and wanted more work with people who liked the convenience of technology and wanted alternatives to the existing transportation offerings. They then executed on that strategy by using tactics to bring it to life. The tactics included: building and perfecting the technology used to connect drivers to passengers; attracting enough drivers in each market; marketing to and building confidence in customers; and addressing the local regulatory challenges in each market.

Do you see the difference? Strategies are the vision and foresight that have to happen, while tactics are the actions we take now. And they both can have a substantial impact on your company. This leak is about all the wasted activity in your organization because people are busy but not productive. They are working but not on the right things.

Are You Too Focused on Tactics Instead of Strategy?

Are you working longer hours than ever? Is your team screaming that they cannot take on another initiative, but you feel you must add more to their plate? Are key priorities getting pushed back because short-term issues keep consuming everyone's time? You may be suffering from being too tactical in your endeavors and not spending enough time on strategizing the plan. If that's the case, let's take a deeper look at exactly why this occurs and how we can put an end to it. At the end of the day this practice results in wasted time, which leads to lost profit or a Leaky Bucket.

Activity Versus Productivity

Organizations lose lots of time and energy running in circles, zig-zagging, and starting and stopping because there was not enough thought invested on the front end to define desired outcomes as well as the best paths to reach them. Could you be guilty of this practice? Are you setting aside at least one day a month and two days a quarter to bring your team together to have strategic discussions? If you are like most, the honest answer is "no!" I am repeatedly told, "We do not have time for meetings; there is too much work, and everyone already knows what must get done." However, this is where you are a danger to yourself and your team. Most likely you are confusing activity with productivity. Activity is just the exertion of energy, and it can be done without any meaningful purpose. But productivity is the exertion of energy to accomplish a very specific goal, which is exactly what we are looking for.

A business owner in the highly competitive information technology services sector provides a great example. When we originally met, he was excited about his business and told me about the initiatives he was implementing to promote growth. His business had plateaued, and he was ready to break the flat revenue pattern. One year after he and I met, I was anxious to hear how the year went. He enthusiastically told me that every initiative worked perfectly. His operation was running really well; his customers were the happiest they had ever been; and his employees were really happy. So then I asked the key question: How was growth? That is when his voice dropped a bit, and his tone changed. He said, "Well, that was not so good." Revenue was at the same level as last year because they had not solved their sales and marketing problem. It didn't surprise me that, even though his new tactics were rolled out, the strategy behind those tactics was not well-considered, or even considered at all. So while his team's attitude had changed, there was no positive impact on the profits. His team had spent long hours working on things that honestly did not matter. Strategically, they were still stuck!

Six Strategic Questions to Ask Constantly

Lack of strategy is an issue for many businesses: They focus on tactics, but not strategies. Everyone loves the moment where the rubber meets the road, but if those tires aren't properly adjusted and connected, your vehicle will quickly fall apart. Leaks occur when strategies and tactics are not harmoniously aligned. A good strategic discussion results in developing better ways of approaching your business. The very best leaders look at how hard everyone is working and then decide there must be a better way.

They require everyone to think about how they approach the business, projects, functions, and to ask questions like:

- What would need to happen to make our sales volume change?
- What would need to happen to inspire people to pay more for our products and services?

- How can we do this with fewer resources?
- How can we do this in less time?
- Why does it have to be done the way we are doing it?
- How can we do it faster, better, and cheaper?

If you do not stop and constantly challenge the team to answer these questions, you may never break bad habits, often start down paths you ought not to travel, and never redirect resources that could be used for higher return priorities, which all cause profit leaks. When you don't ask these questions, you miss the bigger opportunities and confuse being busy with being productive.

A Strategic Shift Can Turn The Tide

A client of mine whose company provided services to people with substance abuse issues offers a great example of the value of strategy. His company was growing and profitable, but cash flow remained tight. The CEO was very unsatisfied with the sales team's performance. By carefully examining the company's internal and external strategies, we increased cash flow by more than $1 million, doubling their sales close ratio in 90 days; reduced their sales team by a third; and completely filled the capacity of their facilities.

Their external strategy was broken because the salespeople were not properly handling their prospects. This made them lose highly qualified, motivated, and referred clients. We learned that the people taking the calls were not connecting with their prospects. Their internal process was antiquated and unnecessarily complex. In order to determine a caller's insurance eligibility, salespeople had to hang up on and then call back potential clients.

After inquiring about what was most important to the prospective client, we concluded that a human element was missing. People wanted assurance that they would receive the care they were calling for. Speed was also essential, because their ideal client had immediate needs to be fulfilled—they required a room in a facility as soon as possible. My client made a few simple changes to their process that had a profound impact.

The biggest change we made happened when we found the company had what was called an "intake form" to collect personal information about a new client. Some salespeople were using this only some of the time—if they had time. We learned from the salespeople that this intake form was not being used because it increased the length of the first call from five minutes to up to an hour. In hindsight it seems crazy. Filling out this form on the first call became a required practice for all salespeople. The completed form was the most important key performance indicator. The connection it created between the person taking the call and the prospect led to increasing closing ratios from 38 percent to 65 percent overnight.

You inquire about the strategy that led to the action. We started with the question: What is most important? Let people know they are cared for! What could happen if an addict hung up the phone? The obvious answer is they could relapse or even worse. So our job was to keep them on the phone and get them into a facility as quickly as possible. It was our purpose to keep them on the road to recovery. The fact that they were calling meant they were on that road. We drove that mindset into every action within the company.

Shift Your Tactical Team to One That Is Strategic

- As Jim Collins taught us in *Good to Great*, the CEO should convene a strategic council for approximately two hours a week with five to twelve people.[48]
- At least one day each quarter should be set aside for strategic thinking.
- Monitor and discuss external trends quarterly to understand how they may suggest underserved opportunities in the market or changes that require you to adjust your business model.
- Meet with customers to unearth new opportunities to add value to customers.
- The leadership team needs to constantly answer these questions:
  1. What are we trying to accomplish? Why?
  2. What areas of the industry are ripe for disruption, and how can you be the organization to cause that disruption?
  3. How are you breaking the rules in your industry?

4. What do your core customers need? Are you addressing their needs well enough?

5. What is your core customer getting from you that your competitors' core customer doesn't yet need?

6. In what areas of your organization could you partner with another organization to better deliver value, dramatically change your cost structure, or invent a new product or service?

7. What item can you eliminate to fund what your core customers really need?

These questions are strategy oriented and certainly require some critical thought. But as you answer each of them, you'll begin to see patterns and recognize your blind spots. This can then lead to a meaningful change in your tactics to create better results for you and your company. If you take strategic thinking seriously, you will recognize that your answers to the same exact questions change over time.

Key Chapter Points
Profit Leak #8: *Focusing on Tactics Instead of Strategy*

- Tactics and strategy are complementary concepts, working together to accomplish goals.
- Strategy defines your ultimate destination or goals for the long term (vision).
- Tactics are the specific actions you'll take to accomplish your strategy.
- Activity is just the exertion of energy, and it can be done without any meaningful purpose.
- Productivity is the exertion of energy to accomplish a very specific goal, which is exactly what we are looking for.
- At least one day each quarter should be set aside for strategic thinking. Look to answer these questions about your business model:
  o What would need to happen to make our sales volume change?

- º What would need to happen to inspire people to pay more for our products and services?
- º How can we do this with fewer resources?
- º How can we do this in less time?
- º Why does it have to be done the way we are doing it?
- º How can we do it faster, better, and cheaper?
- Monitor and discuss external trends quarterly to understand how they may suggest underserved opportunities in the market or changes that require you to adjust your business model.

Chapter 13

PROFIT LEAK #9
Chasing Revenue Everywhere and Anywhere

Y ou should base part of your conversation on strategy on the notion of revenue. Not all revenue is good revenue. Your strategy will help you consider the best type of revenue to target. With that said, let's apply our thoughts on strategy to revenue. The predictability and consistency of your revenue growth rate are important measures of the health of your business. A key to driving your growth is targeting the right market segment, not aiming to be all things to all segments. You might love pie, but you'd likely not be feeling too well if you ate the entire pie at once. The same is true regarding the health of your business. You have to pick the right slice and do so in moderation. Targeting every source of revenue can leave you spread thin, the proverbial jack-of-all-trades and master of none. Profit leaks result from not focusing your efforts on the most valuable and sensible avenues for revenue.

Positioning your company in a growth industry, market segment, or sector is crucial to the continued success of your company. To have future growth, regardless of how you are doing in this quarter or year, there must be a target market that your products/services are focused on and that is regularly growing. When businesses mistakenly chase revenue anywhere it leads them, they wind up with less of it. Great companies quickly learn that by segmenting the marketplace, they can perfect their business model around owning their segment or slice of the pie.

What Is a Segment?

You can become the dominant player in your market sector by focusing your time and effort on a specific customer segment. A segment is a group of customers with common characteristics that influence how they make decisions. In every industry, you can group potential customers into many possible segments.

One segment could consist of buyers who can afford your product or service; another could be people who have an interest in your product or service, or whose similarity is where they might go to buy your product or service, and so on and so forth. Failure to identify segments destroys time allocation strategy in your business when you are not focused on your targeted market. This is more obvious when your company is small and time constraints are more serious. One of my clients has focused on segmenting their market to new homebuyers. Recognizing that this market segment wants the company's product purchased and installed prior to moving into their new homes, they decided to use homebuilders as their sales channel to acquire customers.

In most cases, we consider whether a prospect can afford to do business with us, rather than the likelihood of them actually doing business with us. This is what we call a qualified lead. They are qualified not because they are sure to sign up, but rather because of their ability to sign up if they decide to. When you look at the furniture industry, IKEA mastered focusing on a narrow segment of the market that also happens to be quite large. That is, they segmented their market to target people who want inexpensive, simple furniture that they can easily put together themselves. By focusing only on this segment they built a business model that allowed them to become the world's largest, very profitable furniture retailer.[49]

Narrower Segmentation Is Better

To grow your business faster, you must master how to choose your ideal customer and focus on attracting that kind of customer. The narrower you can make your customer focus, the better. This may seem counterintuitive to the typical entrepreneur, who naturally wants to serve everyone and anyone. The goal of a start-up is more customers, and focus is not usually the topic of discussion. In small businesses, focus is especially hard to consider when revenue may be hard to come by and you may be losing money on a daily basis. However, there are five factors that can help you understand the importance of choosing your customer focus:

1. **Time is limited.**

   You have to consider the purpose you are trying to serve for your customer base. As previously stressed, your company needs to be purposeful. For example, Toyota Motors has done very well over the years. They have done a great job of building very reliable vehicles with a value focus in their Toyota and Lexus brands. In the same industry, Hyundai focuses on a different segment and has worked to make cars more affordable. Both companies have been successful in their own respective ways by targeting very different segments or slices of the industry.[50]

   Each segment you target requires you to spend time to gain their attention. Time spent in front of one segment takes time away from another. In most instances, to properly dominate a segment, you must market and sell to different people in different ways in different places, and all of these people have different expectations and needs. This takes time, and time is finite. By not focusing, businesses harm their growth instead of improving it.

2. **Cash does not grow on trees.**

   To grow your small business, you need to know that cash does not grow on trees, that having cash gives you options, and that you need to use your cash wisely. Going after too many customer segments is not using your cash wisely. You need to understand each segment and where each segment is most likely to buy your product or service. While you may envision a segment as attractive, it becomes much less appealing if you do not have the cash to take the journey. Unfortunately, most business owners do not realize this until it is too late. They throw their cash in lots of directions hoping something will stick. Then they run out of cash or have to settle for a lesser path because they did not have enough foresight to properly choose their ideal customer.

3. **Not all customers are created equal.**

Each segment is not created equal. The harder it is to master a segment, the more valuable it can be to you and your company. The lower the barrier to entry, the more competition you will have, and the less profit you will make. The higher the barrier to entry, the harder it is to acquire the customers, and the more difficult their challenges. The better your ability to master those challenges, the better the opportunity you have for dominance and profit. Your job is to find this segment and to make it easier for your company to dominate by focusing on it.

4. **Complexity.**

For each additional segment you target, every additional product and service line you offer each segment, and the different channels required to reach each segment, you will increase the complexity of your business model.

5. **Channel.**

Each customer segment has a preference for buying your product and service through different sales channels. Too often we "spray and pray" and don't master any of the channels. By understanding your buyer as a person, you can perceive whether they will have a preference to consume your product or service through retail stores, direct sales force, wholesale, partner network, or e-commerce.

This issue is also significant as it relates to cost because you have to consider the cost of acquiring the average customer through each channel. You have to look at the total cost of the channel and not the incremental cost (e.g., sales commission) paid on an individual customer. There is an initial cost as you build the channel and the cost after you have mastered the channel. Sometimes the cost of acquiring customers from a particular channel is too high relative to the gross margin that channel generates. That would make for a bad business model.[51]

Who Do You Target?

You must identify the customers you want a lot more of. When analyzing a company's customer databases, it is not unusual to find that the majority of their revenue is made up of "bad" customers—clients who pay poorly, are less profitable, complain a lot, are hard to service, do not give referrals, etc. This happens mainly because it's easier to get the bad customers when businesses first start and need revenue to survive. This is the low-hanging fruit, and it is also the least juicy.

As companies grow, they continue to use the excuse that they do not feel financially stable enough to focus on getting ideal customers, much less get rid of bad ones. However, it is this lack of focus that drains organizational energy and profits. Furthermore, building a base of bad customers leads to creating a negative image in the marketplace as to who you ought to be serving, and thus a company ends up trapped.

Great companies commit to identifying the best customers and building their strategies around owning that market. By doing so they find that their operation is custom-built toward serving their ideal customer, so they have a competitive advantage. Ideal customers are loyal, so they give you referrals to more ideal customers. All of these customers are more profitable than the other bases of customers that might have been easier to get initially. As you become the leader in the niche, it ultimately becomes easier to attract the ideal client. This leads to a more profitable and stable business model.

Are You Targeting the Right Market Segment?

The predictability and consistency of your revenue growth rate are important measures of the health of your business. A key to driving your growth is targeting the right market segment. Positioning your company in a growth industry, market segment, or sector is crucial to the continued success of your company. To have future growth, regardless of how you are doing this quarter or this year, your products and services must be focused and there must be a growth market in front of you. You know you are in a growth market when the following signals are apparent:

- You can consistently grow your revenue by at least 20 percent per year. More would be preferable.
- Acquiring new customers seems to be easy, and your current quarter compared to the same quarter in the previous year is either the same or growing. Any quarter that shows a dip is a warning sign that an adjustment may be needed.
- Profit margins appear to be holding steady with volume increase. Obvious exceptions to this rule emerge as you hit different steps in expansion.
- You are finding more and more competition in your space. This is why you have to move swiftly and grow quickly when you find a hot market.
- You can find news media, analysts, and industry experts talking about the trends you are taking advantage of. Follow these sources for signs in trend shifts.

Seven Benefits of Choosing the Right Market Segment:
1. Employees. It is easier to attract, keep, and grow the right employees.
2. Customer Acquisition. It is easier to be a winner in a growing market than in one that is declining or stagnant. All boats rise with the tide.
3. Capital. It is easier to attract and lower your cost of capital.
4. Margins. There is a better chance of earning larger profit margins.
5. Operations. Predictable revenue allows you to generate cash and to plan and invest properly in the support structure of your business. This in turn allows you to properly serve your clients.
6. Shareholders. There are higher returns on investment for shareholders.
7. Valuation. Buyers pay more for businesses that are in growth markets.

Five Questions to Help You Choose Your Market Segment

By focusing on a specific customer segment you can become the dominant player in that segment. As we've already noted, a segment is a group of customers with common characteristics that influence how they make decisions. In every industry you can group potential customers into many possible segments. Your leadership team must examine the marketplace and cluster people and organizations into groups, separating them based on common needs, behaviors, or other attributes that your company is equipped to serve. Once you have isolated different groupings, you can look for ways in which they may be underserved today in terms of products or services.

Ask These Five Questions:

1. Do they deserve a distinct offering? How well do your company's current offerings meet their distinct desires and needs?
2. Are they reached through different channels? How well do your current channels work for this grouping?
3. Does this unique set of people or organizations require different types of relationships?
4. How does profitability differ, and could it differ for each grouping? What would need to change to change the game?
5. How much would each grouping be willing to pay for different aspects of the offer?

These are all crucial questions to consider and answer. As business owners, we default to chasing revenue. It is ingrained in our mind and habits. But not all revenue is good revenue, and not all avenues to revenue are paths you should follow. Analyze your best business models and the manner in which you can most reasonably succeed. By looking at revenue as a big pie and determining which slice you want, you'll find it easier to carve out your own piece. If you do not segment, or if you just try to overindulge or spread yourself too thin, you'll find substantial leaks that will cause you to lose valuable time and resources on sure-fire losers.

Key Chapter Points

Profit Leak #9: *Chasing Revenue Everywhere and Anywhere*

- Targeting every possible source of revenue can leave you spread thin, the proverbial jack-of-all-trades and master of none.
  - ○ Profit leaks result from not focusing your efforts on the most valuable and sensible avenues for revenue.
- Great companies quickly learn that by segmenting the marketplace they can perfect their business model around owning their segment or slice of the pie.
- A segment is a group of customers with common characteristics that influence how they make decisions.
- A principle every business owner must master: To help your business grow faster, choose your ideal customer and focus on attracting that kind of customer.
  - ○ The narrower you can make your customer focus, the better.
- You can become a dominant player in your market sector by focusing your time and effort on a specific customer segment.
- Each segment you target requires you to spend time to gain their attention.
  - ○ Time spent in front of one segment takes time away from another.
- To grow your small business, you need to know that cash does not grow on trees, that having cash gives you options, and that you need to use your cash wisely.
  - ○ Going after too many customer segments is not using your cash wisely.
- Each customer segment has a preference toward different sales channels.
  - ○ By understanding your buyer as a person, you can perceive whether they will prefer to consume your product or service through retail stores, direct sales force, wholesale, partner network, or e-commerce.
- You have to look at the total cost of each sales channel and not the incremental cost (e.g., sales commission) paid on an individual customer.

- o Sometimes the cost of acquiring customers from a particular channel is too high relative to the gross margin that channel generates. This makes for a bad business model.
- When businesses first start and need revenue to survive, they are even willing to accept bad customers.
  - o Bad customers are the low-hanging fruit, and also the least juicy.
  - o As companies grow, they continue to use the excuse that they do not feel financially stable enough to focus on getting ideal customers, much less get rid of bad ones.
- Great companies commit to identifying their ideal customers and building their strategies around owning that market.
  - o By doing so they find their operation is custom-built toward serving their ideal customer, so they have a competitive advantage.
- The predictability and consistency of your revenue growth rate are important measures of the health of your business.
- To have future growth, regardless of how you are doing this quarter or year, your products and services must be focused and there must be a growth market in front of you.
- We defined five signals to help you determine if you are in a growth market.
- Choosing the right customer segments benefit: employee acquisition and retention, customer acquisition and retention, your cost of capital, profit margins, operational complexity, shareholder return on investment, and your business valuation.
- We identified five questions to help you choose your market segment(s).

PART IV
EXECUTION LEAKS

*"Ideas are easy. It's the execution of ideas that
really separates the sheep from the goats."*
—Sue Grafton[52]

Chapter 14

PROFIT LEAK #10
Ineffectively Communicating Your Goals and Expectations

I n every survey I have conducted with management teams and employees, the most common and important issue seems to be communication. While everyone is talking, emailing, texting, and sending memos, somehow they are not communicating! Communication is a very challenging aspect in any business, and the larger the company, the more difficult the challenge. Whenever communication breaks down consider it a bucket leak!

Let's use the analogy of a jigsaw puzzle to help you better understand the communication issues within your organization. Puzzles are fun because you start with a picture of what you are going to build. You can assemble the frame and fill in the large hole in the middle. With any new puzzle, you are provided the exact number of pieces, and a picture of the finished product. The colors and shapes help you see where the pieces go. Creating a company is much like building a puzzle, and if you communicate well, the process of assembling the puzzle within your company will ultimately be enjoyable.

Let's throw a few complications into building the puzzle. As a child, I was a bit unorganized and had a number of puzzles. It was not unusual to have puzzle pieces wind up in the wrong boxes, causing me to get close to finishing a puzzle and find a number of pieces missing. In fact, many times my puzzle pieces were kept in a bag because I'd destroyed the box (after all, I was a boy). That left me without the very helpful picture on the front cover to guide me through the process. These obstacles certainly made the process much more difficult. Similar challenges often find their way into business.

Now imagine I gave you a puzzle, but you could not see the front of the box. There were no square edges for you to start on the sides, and to make matters worse, each and every day I threw in some extra pieces that do not belong to the puzzle you are building—or maybe took some away. This is what it feels like to try to build a business when leadership does a poor job of communicating a) its purpose, strategy, goals, and expectations; b) exactly how each department participates; and c) what each person does to contribute to success.

The SMART WAY

Clearly, poor communication leads to profit leaks, and even if your team has every piece of the puzzle, they may not completely recognize how to assemble them. The first step in successfully executing a goal or initiative— the priority—is to state it properly. You know your priority is well-stated when anyone who reads it knows exactly what you are trying to accomplish, and in what time frame. The better a leader states that particular priority, the easier it is to create the action plan. An acronym commonly used for stating a priority properly is:

SMART (Specific, Measurable, Attainable, Realistically High, and Time-Based).

Very briefly, let us discuss what each of these criteria really means:

Specific. Say exactly what it is you want others to do. Hazy goals are doomed to failure. For example, a statement like "We are going to establish a new training program for our supervisors by 10/1/XX" is insufficiently specific. It does not define what you want to train them to do or do differently.

Measurable. The priority must be stated in a way that allows you to definitely know whether it has been achieved. In addition, it's important to identify progress trends so that you can modify your detailed action steps accordingly. For example, a statement like "We are going to increase the frequency of meetings with our hourly staff" is not measurable. Think about how many meetings you have, how many you would consider acceptable, and, during these meetings, what you want to communicate. More importantly, what outcomes do you expect to change by having more meetings? For example, when your hourly employees fill out their culture survey, you want to see that they give a higher rating to being clear on what is expected of them and that they consistently achieve your quarterly department priorities.

Attainable and Realistically High. Goals must be lofty enough so we do not trip over them. If the goal is too low, it will not stimulate anyone to put forth extra effort. On the other hand, if the goal is unrealistically high, no one will take it seriously. You want it high enough so that it challenges the team and motivates them to use resources wisely.

Time-Based. When do you want this priority to be completed? Are there priorities you have talked about for years that are still on your to-do list? Be honest. Likely there are, and it is probably because you have not committed to a deadline. Without the time frame, you cannot determine whether your priority is attainable. Once you have that time frame, you can create your action plan.

Once you have stated your priority in a manner that meets all of the SMART criteria, you need to consider whether they meet the standards known as WAY, an acronym for **W**ritten, **A**ligned, and **Y**ours. This acronym consists of:

Written. Writing down your priorities forces you to clarify your thoughts. So often my clients underestimate the importance of crystalizing what they want. They get impatient and want to quickly move on once we discuss a topic. Ironically, they have a very difficult time describing in 25 words (or hopefully less) what they actually want to accomplish. Imagine if at the point of discussion, you cannot clarify what your thoughts are. Often there is much disagreement in the room and a lack of understanding that has yet to be addressed. There is false consensus on what must be done.

Once written, your priorities serve as a reminder of your objectives, which can keep you and your team focused and motivated among the daily interruptions. When you do not write down your priorities, they somehow change in your proposed time frame, amount, or scope. Verbal priorities, like the stereotypical fish story, have a tendency to shift too easily. Written priorities can promote teamwork and are more easily communicated.

Aligned. Many times priorities meet the SMART criteria on a stand-alone basis but still are not aligned. Once you've written your priorities down, you can review, discuss, and rank them to spot whether they are out of alignment with your strategy. Consider these questions:

- *By achieving your annual priorities will you have made progress toward your three-year strategic priorities?*
- *By achieving your annual priorities will you be making significant progress or resolving the most prominent challenge(s) in your business? Will you have elevated the capabilities of your company to another level?*
- *Are your quarterly priorities moving you toward your annual initiatives? Are there any that are not linked? Does this make sense?*
- *Are individual leader priorities linked to the quarterly and annual priorities of the company? If not, does this make sense?*
- *Do you have too many priorities as an individual, a department, or a company?*
- *Do you have the right resources, and are they available to support your priorities?*

Yours. If a goal is yours, it is much more likely that you will be internally motivated to achieve it. It is hard to get excited about somebody else's goals. When we achieve goals, it increases energy, which has a positive impact on results, thus further increasing energy, increasing focus on goals, increasing results, and so on. It is that simple!

If you want to achieve more goals, make sure you state them in a SMART WAY![53]

Key Questions You Must Answer for Every Employee

With your SMART WAY in hand, you can begin to shift your attention to focusing on communicating with the needs of your employees. If you manage others in your organization, you are responsible for identifying business objectives, establishing a clear set of expected outcomes, creating policies and procedures to guide daily activities, aligning appropriate resources, and providing the development and support necessary to maximize the likelihood that expected outcomes are achieved. As a leader, you have no choice but to consider how you would grade yourself in all of these areas.

Every leader should strive to create an environment that encourages motivation. One of the keys to doing so is being a good manager and working hard to earn an "A" in all the areas of the above responsibilities. My responsibility as an executive coach is to earn an "A" by helping my clients to do so.

Every employee, from the janitor to the CEO, must be able to answer the following two questions. They are the foundation for optimal performance in every company:

1. *Why am I here?*
2. *What is expected of me?*

Why am I here?

This appears to be a simple and harmless question. As discussed in Chapter 12, the typical answers you will hear are variations of "to make money," or a functional person such as a salesperson may respond, "to sell as much business as possible."

While they may be on the right track related to their roles, these answers relate to question number two, not number one. Here we need to address the "purpose" of the organization. From the day someone starts with your company to the day they leave, they must know what that purpose is and how their role contributes to this purpose. Purposeful companies achieve far more with more passionate people than any other organizations on the planet. By selecting a unique, exciting, and compelling purpose, you energize your workforce. This excites everyone about the possibilities that currently do not exist. This creates energy and inspires action.

What is expected of me?

The dynamics of your employee teams are defined by many factors, all of which determine their efficiency and effectiveness. One of the most important factors, in my experience, is defining employee roles. As a leader, you have to communicate clear responsibilities and titles to your team. If not, your team members will overlap and have trouble finding clarity in their specific roles.

How Do You Communicate Expectations?

Let's first address the question of how to communicate our expectations to the employee. For us to be effective, we must properly identify the employee's communication style, which can be categorized as visual, auditory, kinesthetic, or auditory digital.

The visual communicator seeks pictures and often has trouble remembering verbal instructions.

Auditory communicators learn best through listening and can repeat things back to you easily.

Kinesthetic communicators memorize through doing or working through something.

Auditory digital people memorize by steps, procedures, and sequences.[54]

The most important point is that simply providing a job description, no matter how well written and comprehensive, may not be the appropriate means for communicating expectations for every employee.

How Do You Create Role Clarity?

Create a formal, accurate job description. Common pitfalls we see with regard to job descriptions revolve around the fact that many are outdated and really should be reviewed at least once a year. In addition, they cannot be viewed on a singular basis because many people work in and on teams. Failure to synchronize job descriptions can set employees up for failure even when they perform according to their job responsibilities.

Most importantly, employees need to understand and visualize the outcomes that are expected of them. Focusing on measurable outcomes that are aligned with organizational goals has many benefits. First, measurable goals that are aligned with the organization's goals will evolve and change annually in support of the overall business plan. In addition, when employees understand what needs to be accomplished they are in a better position to know how to act independently. Independent thinking promotes problem-solving within the organization, and employees can better prioritize their work and perform more effectively.

Last, these employees will tend to achieve a higher degree of job satisfaction. In our system for Human Capital Management (the process of managing employees from recruitment to retention), we place a huge focus on defining the roles of every employee. This starts with the job posting and carries through into an individual's day-to-day responsibilities. As a business owner, leader, and coach, I have seen firsthand how mindfully defining each employee's role, responsibilities, and success metrics creates success on the team and within the overall company.

Key Components of the Job/Position Profile

Without defining these following position attributes, you are failing to tell employees what they need to accomplish, and without this direction your employees and your team will not deliver the results they could be delivering. This is just one example of communication. Companies literally live and die by their communication channels, whether they recognize it or not. Enormous profit leaks are caused by failures in communication.

Job Description: Collection of tasks and responsibilities that the position entails; includes an official title.

Job Tasks: Unit of work or set of activities needed to produce some result (e.g., answering phones, writing a memo, sorting the mail, etc.).

Job Functions: A group of tasks is sometimes referred to as a function.

Role(s): The set of responsibilities or expected results associated with a job. A job usually includes several roles.

Competencies: Abilities and capacity required to perform the job successfully. Do not confuse competencies with skills. Competencies are abilities you have that cannot be learned, whereas skills can be learned. An example of competency would be "vision."

Performance Management: Provide visibility to performance through the use of metrics and established performance targets, thereby giving context to vague concepts.

Defines how the position's performance is measured and its impact from an organizational perspective.

Key Process Ownership (KPO): Identifies the critical processes owned by the position.

Career History: The background typically required to have gained the level of knowledge, training, range of experiences, and competency required for the position.

Effectively Communicating Your Goals and Expectations

The next three chapters work in tandem with what I have discussed above. Communicating goals and expectations well and aligning them across your organization is hard and critical work. Failure to do so will create a huge leak in your bucket. Making the effort is well worth your time and will avoid unnecessary work and hardship in the long term. Here are actions I suggest you take:

- Create a strategic plan. This forces you to look at your business beyond one year and up to three years out. Defining what your business will look like is critical. If you do not know where your business is headed in the long term you will not know whether your short-term goals and priorities are leading you in the right direction.
- Create an annual business plan. I am not suggesting you write a book. I am simply recommending you have a simple blueprint for how you will elevate your business by the end of the year.

- Do not confuse your business plan with a budget. You cannot create a realistic budget without a specific plan for how you will improve your business fundamentals and model. I have met with many companies that go through phenomenal amounts of detailed modeling to get to precisely the wrong numbers. The leaders have created their numbers without the substance of knowing how they will achieve them.

- Make the plans clear to your team. Once you have created your plans and your goals, everyone in the organization needs to know what their contribution will be to achieving them. Break down expectations (where possible) by week, month, quarter, department, and person. Understand what processes need to improve, what capabilities need to be added, what resources need to be acquired, etc.

- In your meetings, continually discuss progress on your plans and goals.

- On a regular basis, remind everyone of the purpose of your organization and tie everything you do to that purpose.

- For each position, have a position profile that addresses all of the factors addressed above.

- Hold people accountable, a step we'll discuss further in Chapter 16.

Key Chapter Points

Profit Leak #10: *Ineffectively Communicating Your Goals and Expectations*

- While everyone is talking, emailing, texting, and sending memos, somehow they are not communicating! Whenever communication breaks down consider it a bucket leak!

- You know your priority is well stated when anyone who reads it knows exactly what you are trying to accomplish and in what time frame. The better a leader states that particular priority, the easier it is to create the action plan.

- Goals must be SMART (Specific, Measurable, Attainable, Realistically High, and Time-Based).

- Goals must meet the standards known as WAY, an acronym for (Written, Aligned, and Yours).

- If you manage others in your organization, you are responsible for identifying business objectives, establishing a clear set of expected outcomes, creating policies and procedures to guide daily activities, aligning appropriate resources, and providing the development and support necessary to maximize the likelihood that expected outcomes are achieved.

- Every employee must be able to answer the questions, "Why am I here?" and "What is expected of me?"

- Purposeful companies achieve far more with more passionate people than any other organizations on the planet.

- When communicating consider the needs of the visual, auditory, kinesthetic, or auditory digital people.

- Job descriptions should be updated annually and need to be synchronized as employees work in teams.

- Employees need to understand and visualize the outcomes that are expected of them.

- By clearly defining employee roles from the start, not only do we target and hire the best, most qualified candidates, but we ensure their continued success by informing them exactly how that success will be determined and measured.

- We identified the key components of the position profile.

Chapter 15

PROFIT LEAK #11
Emphasizing the Wrong Priorities and Not Aligning the Team

G ood communication is critical to success. The last chapter helped
you recognize that. Furthermore, what you communicate is just as
important as how you communicate. Emphasize the wrong priorities,
and you might get an A+ for communication but an F for the desired outcome.
One trademark of great operations is how well they use time and set priorities.
Setting priorities starts with a plan. A good plan creates focus, sets goals, creates
alignment throughout your organization, and provides a means for accountability.
Have you reduced organizational activity down to the minimum to achieve
maximum results? Are anyone's priorities working at cross-purposes to company
goals? Are your daily activities properly aligned toward your goals? Does your
organization have a "do not do list" and a "do later" list? If you don't address
these issues, you are likely emphasizing the wrong set of priorities to your team.

Many companies do a poor job of creating their plans, costing them serious
growth in revenue and profits, so your annual planning process may need some
fine-tuning. Often, leaders spend too much time talking about goals rather than
on the components of their plan that will help them achieve those goals.

Two indications that your plan needs adjustment are:

- *You do not find the need to visit your plan weekly, monthly, and quarterly with your executive team to make sure you are following it.*
- *You are **not** consistently hitting your revenue and profit numbers on a monthly basis. Or, you **are** hitting those numbers for reasons other than your plan. In other words, you are growing by chance rather than by planned actions.*

Creating a business plan helps your company find the simplest path to produce maximum results. Lack of prioritization is by far the most common issue preventing companies from reaching consistent performance. While most leaders like to blame external conditions, it is usually an internal shortcoming.

To accomplish focus, prioritization, alignment, and accountability, your business plan must clearly answer the following eight concerns:

1. Why do you exist (purpose)?
2. How are you different (unusual offering)?
3. Who is the core customer you will build your business around?
4. What are your goals?
5. Which "Critical Numbers" will you elevate this quarter?
6. What are your three to five essential annual priorities? Remember, these are the difficult changes that need to be made in terms of products and services, systems and process, and people.
7. What are the three to five quarterly company priorities that will drive the annual priorities?
8. What are the three to five quarterly personal priorities for every leader that align with the company priorities and functional priorities?[55]

Prioritizing Your Annual Initiatives

Planning requires prioritizing initiatives. This will help you send the right message to your team and prevent time and resource losses. As with most plans, no more than five annual initiatives are recommended—fewer is preferred. Once you have your Critical Numbers, which we'll discuss in

Chapter 17, you can determine which initiatives are most important to undertake, maintaining at least one annual initiative focused on just your Critical Number(s).

Most leaders fail to create a good business plan. The secret is in the annual initiatives. Many leaders confuse business planning with budgeting. Others confuse action steps with priorities or initiatives. Some are not thinking big enough when creating their plans. Are you finding it challenging to create a good business plan? How often is there a difference between the plan you created and the actions your team initiates? How big is the gap between expected and actual performance? In my experience, poor business planning may cost you serious growth in revenue and profits.

A good business plan helps you determine the three to five annual initiatives that move your business forward. Many business leaders ignore their weakness in this area because they might not understand their direct impact to their financial goals. Annual priorities are usually strategic in nature and do not show directly in the profit and loss report (P & L), such as initiatives that strengthen customer loyalty. The natural tendency is to worry about today, which is why most business plans are never executed.

Common Business Plan Pitfalls

- *Poor Clarity.* An initiative should be described with such clarity that a stranger would know what you are trying to accomplish and be able to hold you accountable.
- *Short-Term Focus.* Some plans focus on initiatives that affect only the most immediate quarterly goals. Every business needs to make money and cover its expenses, but problems occur when you are so focused on the short term that you are not able to make the changes necessary for making quantum leaps.
- *Ignore the Trends.* Many leaders continue to ignore the fact that the traditional ways in which their customers purchase their products and services have changed. Blockbuster didn't recognize these emerging trends and was replaced by forward-thinking companies like Netflix.

- *Accepting Your Weaknesses.* Knowing that you have weaknesses is not the same as doing something about them. Make it a priority to seriously address, if not eliminate, at least one weakness per year.
- *Overambition.* Too often leaders see all the things they are unhappy with and try to turn them all into priorities. Generally, it is good practice to have five or fewer annual priorities. I prefer three.

Quarterly Priority Planning

While many companies create an annual business plan, quarterly planning sessions often maintain focus and alignment with longer-term initiatives. It is great to have an annual plan, but it is essential that everyone in the organization have clarity on quarterly goals. Each thirteen13-week cycle (90 days or quarter) is an essential building block for a successful year. Stated simply, failure to have the right priorities or to follow through leads to lower results.

The most successful leaders realize that to move their businesses forward they must immediately move on their highest priorities. This may sound basic, but most organizations fail to achieve their annual initiatives, and a primary reason is failure to master each quarter. Procrastination is the biggest issue. Typically, leaders underestimate the amount of effort, time, and obstacles they are going to encounter to achieve their initiatives. As a result, they get started too late, if at all.

To assist clients in their quarterly planning, I frequently use the Gazelles One-Page Strategic Plan created by Verne Harnish and discussed in great detail in his book, *Scaling Up*. I work with clients to develop quarterly "rocks." These are the three to five most important priorities for the company, the ones that must be met in the next 90 days. By helping the management team agree on these priorities, you can increase intensity and focus on what matters most for business. When leaders try to make everything equally important, they end up highlighting nothing. The more you can focus your people around specific priorities, the more traction you will gain toward accelerating the growth of your business.[56]

"Rock" is a term I've intentionally used interchangeably with "initiative." You may have read about this in Stephen Covey's book *First Things First*, or have seen the following exercise performed in a leadership or time-management training program you attended. Picture a glass jar on a table. Next to it you have large rocks, gravel, sand, and water. The leadership trainer typically fills the jar with the big rocks first and asks the group if the jar is full. Everyone says it is. The trainer then pours gravel into the jar and shakes it around to fill in all the holes and again asks, "Is this jar full?" Of course, there is now reluctance to answer. Next, the trainer takes the sand and pours it into the cracks in the jar and asks again, "Is this jar full?" Finally, the trainer adds the water. The object of the demonstration is for you to recognize that the rocks are your main priorities; the gravel represents your day-to-day responsibilities; the sand stands for interruptions; and the water is everything else you get hit with during your workday. If you are like most people, you would pour the water in first, the sand in second, the gravel in third, and the rocks last. The lesson: There will be no room for anything else unless you first put the rocks in the container.[57]

When setting your quarterly rocks, here are a few things to consider:

- **Linkage to Annual Priorities**: Ideally your rocks are linked to your annual priorities.
- **Focus on Higher Priorities:** Make sure you have more activities leading toward bigger/higher-impact rocks.
- **Communicate Your Rocks**: Make sure everyone knows what the rocks are and understands how they are aligned with the company.
- **Track Progress:** Discuss status and progress on your rocks weekly to make sure they are getting the proper attention and resources.

Quarterly planning is not as easy as it appears. Some tough tradeoffs happen. Many times it is hard to see the excuses because all the members of the team are stuck in the same sand and water. This is where a good business coach can make a difference.

Key Chapter Points
Profit Leak #11: *Emphasizing the Wrong*
Priorities and Not Aligning the Team

- A good plan creates focus, sets goals, creates alignment throughout your organization, and provides a means for accountability.
- Leaders spend too much time focusing their attention on goals rather than on the components of their plan that will help them achieve those goals.
- If you do not find the need to visit your plan weekly, monthly, and quarterly with your executive team to make sure you are following it . . . you do not have one.
- If you are not consistently hitting your revenue and profit numbers on a monthly basis your plan is flawed and needs to be adjusted.
  - If you are hitting your goals for reasons other than your plan, don't let yourself off the hook.
- Creating a business plan helps your company find the simplest path to producing maximum results.
- Planning requires prioritization of initiatives.
- Annual priorities such as initiatives that strengthen customer loyalty are usually strategic in nature and do not show directly in P & L statements.
  - The natural tendency is to worry about today, which is why most business plans are never executed.
- We identified eight concerns to help you accomplish focus, prioritization, alignment, and accountability.
- It all starts with three to five annual initiatives that move your business forward that are strategic in nature.
- The five common business planning pitfalls are poor clarity, short-term focus, ignoring trends, acceptance of your weaknesses, and overambition.
- Get your 13-week race right! If you do not have a quarterly plan that will immediately rally your organization around your annual priorities, you are going to fail in achieving them.
- The time it takes for planning far outweighs the problems created when you don't.

---- *Chapter 16* ----

PROFIT LEAK #12
Being Allergic to Saying "No"

I f you are communicating well, you are emphasizing messages you really want your team to hear. One message that should be absolutely clear is the right type of opportunities you expect your team to aggressively pursue. To a very large degree, your success will depend on whether you master the art of effective time organization. To do that, you must pick and choose which opportunities and tasks to undertake. Time management is a skill few people master, but every person needs. One of the greatest mistakes many leaders make is to say "yes" too often. In many cases, time management is more about what you decide *not* to do, rather than what you actually do. Does your leadership team fail to say "no" often enough? Or does it choose to chase fires rather than identify and address the real issues staring them in the face? While there is no exact percentage, you should be passing on at least 25 percent of the opportunities and responsibilities that come your way. Otherwise, you will find yourself spending far too much time on tasks you never should have agreed to take on in the first place.

Do You Use Your Time or Does Your Time Use You?

You cannot manage time itself, but you can manage how you choose to use your time. We are under more time pressure than ever, and those little gadgets like cell phones may actually make our lives much harder than easier.

Time is the great equalizer. Everyone gets the same amount of time: 24 hours in each day. You cannot buy more time, and no one can give you more of it. Thus, the most important question you can ask daily is: "How can I and my team use time more wisely?"

One of the essential keys to maximizing success as an individual or an organization is to effectively determine where your time should go now and into the future. Where you used time in the past only serves as a guide, a learning mechanism for your decisions as to where time should be used in the future. One person in your group losing focus on congruent goals can impact everyone's time and even create a huge barrier to success.

Too often people search in the wrong places when trying to understand why they are not achieving their goals. They think there is something wrong with the time management program they're using, so they buy a new one. The real problem is not what program or process they currently use. Rather, it is what habits of thoughts and attitudes they use to decide how they will use their time.

Belief systems lead to actions that cause results, which then impact your time management. If you or your people behave in counterproductive ways, try to identify what the belief systems are that cause that behavior. For example, let's say you decide you should exercise three days a week to improve your health. Your primary belief system, however, is that exercise is boring and painful. What do you think the chances are you'll implement that "decision" to exercise three days a week?

Commonly, I hear CEOs complain that they spend little or no time on their strategic priorities. Instead, they spend their days putting out fires and dealing with their employee issues. They are usually insistent this is just part of business as usual. However, a closer examination teaches us that some people like to put out fires. They enjoy the immediate gratification of handling the daily emergencies, want to be the ones with all the answers, and have trouble saying "no" to others. These habits directly impact their ability to manage their time effectively.

Our society is notorious for seeking immediate gratification. The benefit of better health is a long-term goal. In the short term, however, a person is apt to avoid the pain of sore muscles and the loss of self-esteem that goes along with confirming one's own bad physical shape by not going to the gym. In other words, they feel better about not going to the gym than they do about going. This is immediate gratification, even though the decision is a bad one for long-term goals.

To change behavior, you must identify the immediate gratification you get from your bad behavior and the thought patterns that cause you to continue to practice it. Once identified, you must find something more motivating to replace them. For example, many people would exercise if their doctor told them, "If you do not start to regularly exercise tomorrow, you'll have only six months to live. If you do exercise regularly, you will live another twenty-five years." That is quite a carrot to dangle.

An additional aspect of using time is that most people do not have a good sense of where their time goes. At least once every six months, executives should track their time to see where they really spend it. Once you have a solid understanding of how you spend your time, you can redirect time you control and use it more productively by delegating activities to others.

Without Saying No, Everything Is Equally Important

You set your employees up for failure by saying yes to everything. When everything is important, nothing is truly important! Perfection does not exist. Simple math dictates that the more things you randomly throw on someone's plate, the more overloaded they get. Overloads cause leaks in company buckets.

A domino effect occurs when leaders cannot say "no" to anything. Let's take the people ramifications. The more complicated your service model, the more talented your service staff has to be. They have to be smarter than the average employee in the marketplace while also maintaining specialized skills to handle your customers. That said, when you overload them with responsibilities, you'll find they cannot reach all of your original projected goals.

You can reduce complexity by saying "no."

A great example of a company that benefited from saying "no" is Southwest Airlines. They say "no" often. If you want reserved seating, you do not fly Southwest, because their boarding process does not allow for it. Southwest Airlines, unlike most of the competition, does not charge for bags. As mentioned in an earlier chapter, all of their planes are 737s. This simplifies their fleet, reduces the time it takes to train mechanics, and drastically improves inventory management. In addition, they do not provide onboard amenities. Also, you will notice they fly to fewer than 100 destinations. They choose airports with lower gate fees. Additionally, you can only book flights on their website. The culmination of all of these "no" decisions is that they have remained one of the most profitable airlines in the industry and as of this writing are second only to Delta Airlines in market capitalization with approximately half the number of employees.[58]

Saying "No" Will Simplify Your Life

Typically, leaders push back on the concept of saying "no". To that end, make it a priority NOT to schedule any meetings or calls in the first three hours of each day. Use that time to work on one key task to move the rocks out of your way. If you finish in less time, use the leftover time to go after the gravel, sand, and water tasks (in that order), which also fill your daily bucket. This ensures you are working on at least five key motivators each week. You have been trained since you entered the workforce to please your customers and your bosses. They make you feel as if you always have to go the extra mile and exceed expectations! The problem with this mentality is that by trying to please everyone, you end up pleasing no one. You set yourself and others up for failure. You might think it takes courage to say "no". In reality, it takes brains to say "no". And the better practice is to prioritize your time commitments and always put thoughtful productivity at the forefront of your mind.

Key Chapter Points
Profit Leak #12: *Being Allergic to Saying "No"*

- Time management is more about what you decide not to do, rather than what you actually do.
- Saying yes too often could be the main reason why time may be using you instead of you using time.
- You cannot manage time itself, but you can manage how you choose to use your time.
- One of the essential keys to maximizing success as an individual or an organization is to effectively determine where your time should go now and into the future.
- Belief systems lead to actions that cause results, which then impact your time management.
- To change behavior, you must identify the immediate gratification you get from your bad behavior and the thought patterns that cause you to continue to practice it.
- At least once every six months, executives should track their time to see where they really spend it.
  - Once you have a solid understanding of how you spend your time, you can try to increase the amount of time you control and use it more productively by delegating activities to others.
- When everything is important, nothing is truly important!
- Without saying no, everything is equally important. You do not have infinite time.
- Saying no more often will simplify your life.
- Conduct a 30-minute weekly review of your accomplishments from the prior week and spend time using them to plan out the following week. A weekly personal planning process like this can help you evaluate how to spend your time.

Chapter 17

PROFIT LEAK #13
Monitoring the Wrong Numbers

C ommunicate, then emphasize. But always monitor if the message is hitting close to home. That is the focus of this chapter. As with time management, many companies do not pay enough attention to goal setting. In fact, many organizations set goals and fail to reach them. Others achieve some of their goals by accident. Some leaders question whether setting goals is a valuable exercise at all. Adam Galinsky, a professor at Northwestern University's Kellogg School of Management and one of the authors of a Harvard Business School report called *Goals Gone Wild*, argues that "goal setting has been treated like an over-the-counter medication when it should really be treated with more care, as a prescription-strength medication." He argues that goal setting can focus too much attention on the wrong things and can lead people to participate in extreme behaviors to achieve their goals.[59]

I believe goal setting serves a critical purpose in providing direction, clarifying priorities, prompting important discussions, influencing positive behavior change, and stimulating focus. Goals are an essential part of the time/strategy equation. However, like anything else in life, goal setting will not serve the intended purposes and can cause more harm than good if it is developed in an unsound way, misdirected, overemphasized, and not used in context.

It is important to establish balanced goals. Often, people do not put enough thought into their goals and leave them incomplete. One of my clients was so focused on achieving a sales goal every year that he never even came close to reaching it. It was not until he had a complete set of goals that he ever made real sales progress. When focused correctly, goals take into account customers, employees, shareholders, vendors, operations, sales, profit, and recordkeeping.

Have you developed your goals in a sound way? Often goals are arbitrary. You may be missing your goals every year because there is little basis for how you developed them. Are you capturing random numbers in a spreadsheet or pulling numbers from thin air? Are your goals really dreams or wishes? The only difference between real goals and dreams is an action plan!

What to Consider When Setting Your Revenue Goal

Have you thought through what it would take to achieve your annual revenue goal? Have you answered questions such as:

- Will pricing need to stay the same, increase or be decreased?
- Which customers will grow, and which will be lost?
- Why will certain customers grow? Will it be due to price increases, greater purchase volume, or an expansion of our product lines or services?
- How many sales will come from new customers? How many new customers would be needed to reach the goal? How much on average will each of these customers spend? What will they buy?
- Will you need to enter new territories?
- Do you have enough salespeople?
- Do your current salespeople have the right skills and connections?
- Will you need new sales channels?
- Will you need to offer new product or service lines?

Why Do Goals Matter?

Goals direct you and your team toward the right priorities. By identifying gaps between current performance and your goals, you can focus on the gaps and increase the likelihood of desired outcomes. Goals allow you to consolidate your efforts away from activities that are not going to produce the results you want. Your action plan is developed from the answers derived from asking the right questions about how to close the gap.

Goals can rally an organization to extraordinary results. Do you remember the insurance company from the very beginning of the book? Their goal of reducing 35,000 hours became a centering point for leadership team to rally around and aligned the entire organization. They never would have gotten the results they did had they not started by setting the goal.

Be Careful When Setting Your Goals

The opposite can also occur when an organization focuses too much on the wrong goals. Usually the "wrong" goal is sales growth, the thought process being that increased sales solve all problems. However, not all sales are created equal. In many cases transactions and customers can be unprofitable. As previously discussed, you have to focus on the right type of customer. People who try to "make it up on volume" typically lose.

Goals can lead to extreme behaviors and can be destructive if misdirected. One common mistake is the sales team discounting products and services to close deals at the end of a quarter simply to meet their quarterly revenue target and push up volume. Putting this into context, you are paying someone extra to earn you less money! This can cost you in a number of ways:

1. You make less profit in the long term, assuming you could have closed the same transaction for more by waiting.
2. You train your customers to expect that your pricing is not firm, that they can squeeze better pricing out of your salespeople if they wait until quarter end.
3. You are not training your salespeople to maximize margin at every turn. In the end you may sell more but make less.

4. You pay commission on lower dollar deals and applaud your salesperson for a great job.
5. The incremental transactions push you into the next bonus category, and you reward the management team for encouraging the lower-margin deals.

Another critical issue is how to respond when a goal is not achieved. Too often, people perceive goals as optional. Sometimes goals are achieved, but the desired actions by team members are not. Other times, goals are missed because your assumptions in developing them were incomplete or wrong. Depending on your culture, the attitudes toward goals could actually lead people to perform poorly.

Responding to Gaps and Shortfalls?

Your response to missed goals will define you as a leader. Are you thoughtful before you respond, or do you regularly punish and criticize people for missing goals, regardless of the situation? Do you treat everyone equally, or do you have favorites? Do you consider how people achieved their goals and address people who underachieved? Do you evaluate the initial assumptions that caused you to arrive at particular goals and compare them to actual circumstances? Leaders who consistently handle this issue poorly eventually lose the respect of others, reduce motivation, and hold back the company.

By not monitoring the achievement of goals, or failing to address gaps, a leader prevents the organization from learning. Moreover, that leader will not learn what the issues and possibilities are and who the real performers are. Missing goals are necessary steps in the learning process. Goals are meant to be a means to an end—not to be an end in themselves. No one enjoys failing to achieve a goal. Your progress is determined by how you respond. In the end, a nonresponse encourages mediocrity or apathy toward your goals.

Knowing the Difference Between Leading and Lagging Indicators

For most leaders, the primary metrics used to set goals and manage the business come from the income statement and balance sheet. Examples most often discussed are sales, cost of goods sold, gross margin, overhead, labor costs, profit, receivables, inventory, work-in-process, payables, and cash. While you need to monitor these measures, they are all lagging indicators. They are results from decisions and actions taken in the past. They comprise the scorecard you use to measure the success of those actions and decisions. The problem with using these measures to manage the business is that they come after the fact. While there is some benefit to using lagging information, it does not tell you why your results are the way they are. It is also too late to change the outcome. It is the equivalent of driving your car by looking in your rearview mirror.[60]

Focus your primary key performance indicators on leading measures that influence your lagging results the most. By choosing the right leading indicators, you can help your team improve the lagging indicators. This is problematic for leaders for three reasons. First, while all numbers on your balance sheet and income statement are lagging indicators, other measurements can be leading or lagging, depending on what you are using them for. For example, "Percentage of "A" players" can be a lagging indicator when measuring effectiveness of recruiting and onboarding processes, leadership effectiveness, and how well an employee is performing. Conversely, it can be a leading indicator when used to calculate customer loyalty, labor efficiency ratios, and other such measures. Clearly, it is important to isolate what you are trying to improve.

Find Your Biggest Leaks and Narrow Your Focus

The second challenge is determining which measurements require the most attention. Every business is a compilation of processes that encompass various inputs, outputs, and decision points. Each point to when something occurs or doesn't. This will influence future outcomes and can potentially be measured. If yours is like many businesses, your processes may not be well defined, which adds a huge leak to your bucket. Also, you may not be clear on what the impact of each process point has on the overall organization.

In the restoration industry, for example, paperwork is a big issue. If the water technicians do not get their paperwork right and processed timely it impacts their company's ability to receive future assignments from a carrier, and affects profit margins, customer satisfaction, accurate billing, and speed of collections. So a huge emphasis must be placed on perfect paperwork. This is a key measurement that many companies fail to track closely. It would be a great idea to track winning streaks of technicians producing perfect daily paperwork for the most consecutive days. Have an award every time someone sets a record.

What to Do When Measurements Are Not Easily Available

The third issue is the measurement itself. While there are usually systems and processes in place to compile your financial statements, many small and midmarket companies do not have methods for measuring their processes. As a result, there is uncertainty as to how to get the information you need and whether it will be accurate.

The bottom line is still "What gets measured gets done." You do not want to measure too many things. If you cannot automate, have the people responsible for the outcome or the steps in the process report measure their results daily. Set up a manual system where they are required to record their results every day. Many of my clients collect information in Google Docs or in some central repository for information. While this is less than ideal because it is manual and requires an honor system, it does work. If you do not measure, things will not improve.

Finding Your Critical Numbers

As a business coach I have created and reviewed hundreds of annual business plans. Many companies do a poor job of creating their plans, which seriously diminished their growth in revenue and profits. On the surface, all these plans looked like they had the right ingredients for success. However, a closer look showed that the leaders hadn't covered all the bases. Then they lost valuable time and energy, creating a profit leak.

As a certified Gazelles coach, I help clients implement the concepts found in *Scaling Up*. Its "One-Page Strategic Plan" is a key tool everyone looks forward to using in our annual planning process.[61] Whether your company uses this business planning tool or something else, you must still consider the same issues. It's only the presentation of the business plan that is different.

At the bottom of each of the "priorities" columns of the "One-Page Strategic Plan" is the "Critical Number" section. Selecting the Critical Number is one of the single most important decisions in the planning process. The Critical Number is a key performance indicator you have identified as the essential leading indicator for that planning period. Whether you are planning the year, the quarter, or your personal priorities, it is essential to pick the one or two Critical Numbers that must be achieved to drive all of the other desired outcomes. If you are not sure which Critical Numbers to select, you'll find some clues by asking yourself questions like:

- What is the key weakness in our business model?
- What is the biggest weakness in our operations?
- What is causing us not to gain customers?
- What is causing us to lose customers?
- What is causing our cost structure to be out of line with our competitors'?

Revenue is a common number clients want to use. It is not a good choice for a Critical Number. If growth is an issue, you need to go deeper and find the leading indicator at the root of that problem. For example, are you not able to generate enough leads? Do you generate enough quality leads?

I encountered a great example of failure to identify the correct Critical Number in a technology company that recently ran into trouble. The company was mildly successful for years and realized moderate revenue growth and great profit margins, yet it always experienced inconsistent performance from its sales team. Meeting revenue targets often depended on a yearly home-run sale. There was no predictability in sales performance.

Recently the company found that making sales was becoming more challenging and customers now preferred the products of competitors. After deep consideration, the company realized it was not delivering on its number one brand promise. I had challenged this client a few years ago to institute more specific measurements of their brand promises. They had failed to do so, and now this had come back to haunt them. Believe it or not, the number one brand promise they were failing to meet was that their product could do what it was supposed to do. My client was failing to "get it right." So we developed a way to measure the "number of known issues unsolved" within their technology. That became their Critical Number.

Once you find your Critical Number, ask the question, "If we focus too much on this Critical Number, what could go wrong in the company?" If the answer is nothing, then you only need that one Critical Number. However, if you determine that focusing on that number hurts other areas of the business, you'll want to balance the first Critical Number with a second one. This will prevent you from unintentionally injuring your progress. In the case above, the company had a cash concern. Its main issue was the speed of closing deals in the pipeline. So the team focused on the number of transactions that could be accelerated that quarter as its second Critical Number. In both cases my client's focus on the issues solved both problems.

As you can see, prioritizing your leading indicators will help you send the right message to your team and prevent the waste of time and resources. Most of the organizations I've dealt with either fail to have a good understanding of their numbers or are trying to monitor too many. Again, less is more. Having a good handle on what to monitor daily, weekly, and monthly will help you focus on the business. There will be certain key performance indicators the executive team will monitor. Subject matter and functional experts have their own role-specific indicators to watch to know whether they had a good day or good week.

Key Chapter Points
Profit Leak #13: *Monitoring the Wrong Numbers*

- Goal setting serves a critical purpose in providing direction, clarifying priorities, prompting important discussions, influencing positive behavior change, and stimulating focus.
- You may be missing your goals every year because there is little basis for how you developed them.
- The only difference between real goals and dreams is an action plan!
- By identifying gaps between current performance and your goals, you can focus on those gaps and increase the likelihood of desired outcomes.

- Your response to missed goals will define you as a leader.
    - Leaders who consistently handle this issue poorly eventually lose the respect of others, reduce motivation, and hold back the company.
- By not monitoring the achievement of goals, or failing to address gaps, a leader prevents the organization from learning.
- Lagging indicators are results from decisions and actions taken in the past.
    - The problem with using these measures to manage the business is that they come after the fact.
    - While there is some benefit to using lagging information, it does not tell you why your results are the way they are.
    - Lagging indicators leave you no time to change the outcome.
- By choosing the right leading indicators, you can help your team improve the lagging indicators.
- It has been said, "What gets measured gets done!"
- Find your critical numbers and make them your priority.
- It is better to measure something and be directionally correct than not measure at all.

———| *Chapter 18* |———

PROFIT LEAK #14
Ineffective Meetings or Lack of Meetings

O   ftentimes, regular meetings are the best way to ensure you are correctly
         measuring your progress. However, these meetings must be purposeful,
         thoughtful, and useful. Whether you like it or not, meetings are vital
to running your organization. Show me a business without meetings, and I will
show you how it is destined for failure. At best, a no-meeting company will leak
valuable resources like time and money.

Well-executed meetings can accelerate and improve the decision-making
process, align the team, improve prioritization, and make communication more
efficient. When done poorly, meetings do none of these things.

Do you feel like you spend too much time in meetings? Do you talk about
the same problems over and over? When you are in meetings, do they feel
unnecessarily long? Do you talk about a lot of issues but really make no decisions?
It is common to hear leaders express these complaints and not look forward to
meetings. It's less common when leaders look forward to their meetings and exit
them feeling thankful they had the meeting in the first place. So the real question
is: What does your company's meeting structure look like?

Here are eight factors that can improve your meetings:

1. Welcome constructive conflict.
2. Focus on purpose rather than agendas.
3. Set aside enough time to achieve your purpose.
4. Establish proper meeting rhythms.
5. Start meetings on time and keep commitments.
6. Measure the success of each meeting.
7. Select your attendees properly.
8. Avoid the three most common meeting pitfalls.

Welcome Constructive Conflict

Are your meetings boring? How many meetings does it take before you can make a key decision? Are your meetings mainly status updates? Do one or two leaders dominate the meetings? Is the senior leader dictating to everyone else what they must do? How well aligned are everyone's priorities? Do leaders hold each other accountable? Do all the leaders really say what they are thinking? Are everyone's ideas heard? Do people leave feeling stressed? If your meetings fit these descriptions, they could be a lot more productive than they are currently.

A strong leading indicator of a great meeting is when something important is discussed and improved upon via opinions and conflict. It is a bad sign when you are the only one considering the options for an important decision. It means you have not really engaged the rest of the team in those decisions. You have dictated a decision rather than engaged everyone to make one. This behavior implies that leaders believe the rest of the team has nothing of value to add to the decision, and they are smarter than everyone else in the room.

A good meeting increases your options in making a decision, influences new actions for your company, increases the number of new ideas for addressing problems and challenges, and elevates the percentage of goals achieved. Participant input is a real indicator that your meetings are worthwhile. When you have a really good meeting, everyone leaves feeling invested in the decisions made and aligned as a team! If you run your meeting well, participants leave feeling stretched but not stressed.

Healthy conflict is a sign of a good meeting because it helps people venture out of their comfort zones. Do not confuse this with stress. A proper meeting environment allows everyone to do their best thinking. When there is a lack of conflict or engaged dialogue among the team members, it indicates you are not talking about anything that requires any real discussion. Additionally, you are failing to emphasize the hard-to-achieve goals and key performance indicators, not holding people accountable, and not talking about the elephants in the room or the real issues going on in the company. If your meetings do not have this type of regular conflict, you have a problem with your team. The lack of conflict can be an indication that the foundation of a strong team—trust—is missing.

Is 50 percent or more of your meeting time gobbled up by status updates? Status updates are not a great use of time and should take up no more than 15 percent of your meetings. During status updates, attention must be given to accountability issues. When people are off track, discuss what they can change to get back on track with their committed priorities. Often when status updates identify that people are off track, there is not enough inquiry from the other leaders to understand why a fellow teammate is letting down the team and how that is going to change.

Focus on Purpose Rather than Agendas

Do you want to increase the effectiveness of your meetings? Do you ever wonder whether you belong at a particular meeting? Do you ever wonder what the difference is between one meeting and another? Is it possible you talk about too many topics at your meetings and don't delve deep enough into any of them?

Defining the purpose of a meeting and naming the meeting based on that purpose allows leaders to gain clarity on who needs to be at the meeting and what agendas are to be addressed. At the end of the meeting, everyone can answer the question, "Did we achieve our purpose?"

For example, let's say you need to hold a meeting to decide whether to acquire a company called Blue Diamond. You could name the meeting "Pros and Cons of Acquiring Blue Diamond." Everyone invited knows they will be involved in deciding whether to acquire Blue Diamond, and everyone will be expected to be prepared. Attendees will have to decide what information needs to be prepared prior to the meeting and by whom. Giving focus to the meeting, declaring its purpose, and making sure people are prepared for the discussion leads to much better dialogue and faster resolution. If at the end of the meeting you still can't make the decision, then determine what specific action steps are needed to make that decision and what alternative decision deadline is acceptable.

Consistently using the approach of naming and setting a purpose for your meetings will help you determine if your meetings are effective, as well as how often your meetings fail to achieve their purpose and why. If not reaching a decision is a regular occurrence, challenge your team to identify whether a failure in preparation or some other symptom is causing the organization to be ineffective. Don't let yourselves off the hook.

Set Aside Enough Time to Achieve Your Purpose

Does your organization face the same problems and challenges year after year, with no resolution? Do you discuss the same issues, concerns, people, and customers month after month? Do you find that just when you get to the heart of the matter in an important debate or topic your meeting is over and you have to postpone to some later date? Do you create goals and plans that do not come to fruition? These are typical results when you do not spend enough time meeting with your leadership team.

Have you considered the amount of time, productivity, and growth you have lost by not setting aside the time to properly make decisions, to debate and resolve issues, to align priorities and to hold leaders accountable? Avoiding meetings leads to critical decisions not getting made, getting made poorly, or getting made unilaterally. Failure to debate priorities and work through issues can bring organizations to a standstill while leaders wait until the next meeting or for a final decision, allowing your competition the opportunity to thrust forward. While it is counterintuitive to most leaders, spending more time in meetings could actually double or triple company productivity.

Making a commitment to set aside enough time to complete the stated agenda is key. Be sure the executive team is allocating the appropriate time blocks to work on the business, to debate issues focused on strategy, accountability, setting priorities, new opportunities, evaluating your people, challenging the business model, etc.

A key lesson here: Be realistic when setting aside time and use that time wisely. If you are going to discuss an acquisition that could double the size of your company, carve out more than fifteen minutes of your day to do so. Prior commitments to lower-impact issues might have to be set aside when big opportunities present themselves and require the team to assemble.

Proper Meeting Rhythms

Focusing your meetings around decisions and the nature of the decisions to be made, help determine the number of meetings to schedule. Highly effective organizations have learned to schedule a gtood series of daily "huddles" and weekly, monthly, quarterly, and annual meetings that can be carefully designed to get all of the right people together at the same time. Each meeting is assigned a purpose built around specific decisions to be made. Then the agenda is constructed to facilitate making those decisions and encourages the dialogue necessary to reach those decisions. The outcomes of these meetings then become policies and actions that need to be taken as a result of those decisions.

As pointed out in Pat Lencioni's book *Death by Meeting*, most leaders think they have too many meetings.[62] The real issue is that they conduct or attend too many bad meetings. Is it your habit or preference to meet people one-on-one to get their ideas on major issues? If so, that's unfortunate because experience shows that to be very ineffective habit. You wind up repeatedly discussing the same issue without really creating the right debate, fluidity, and speed appropriate to the matter.

Companies that allocate the following time blocks for meetings communicate and execute better with less effort than their peers:

- 7–15 minutes a day for a huddle with your direct team
- Weekly Meeting: ½–1½ hour per week
- Monthly Meeting: ½–1 full day
- Quarterly Meeting: 1½–2 days[63]

Start Meetings on Time and Keep Commitments

Are you in the habit of keeping your time commitments? When you are scheduled to attend a meeting or conference call, are you early, just in time, casually late, known to reschedule often, or known for being habitually late? If you are honest, your real answer will be, "it depends." It depends on who you are meeting with; the purpose of the meeting; how important the meeting is to you; whether you feel the group will wait for you or start without you; your seniority as compared to the others in the room; whether there any consequences for lateness; whether you think what you are doing is more important than what will happen at the meeting, etc. In other words, it's all about YOU, and you are being selfish. Does it matter that you do not care about the feelings of others, are only worried about the here and now, and are not thinking about the broader consequences? Yes, it does.

Every time you reschedule, cancel, miss, or are late to a meeting, you generate direct or indirect costs and resources. If you look at the situation objectively and follow the chain of impact from rescheduling, canceling, missing, or being late to quantify the costs, you would see that some examples include:

- Reduced employee loyalty and satisfaction because of frustration, disappointment, or even anger, which in turn leads to decreased productivity or increased employee turnover.
- Reduced customer loyalty and satisfaction because of frustration, disappointment, or even anger, which decreases revenue.
- Increased errors, which can reduce customer service or product quality, leading to a rise in product returns, reduced revenue, increased chargebacks, etc.
- Decreased productivity while people wait around for meetings to start, or sit through recaps of material already covered for the benefit of latecomers.
- Increases in the length of time it takes to make critical decisions, sometimes by months, which costs you revenue and even extra expenses.

In my experience, the culprits always justify their actions with comments such as:

- "It was a sales opportunity."
- "My biggest customer needed me."
- "An emergency had to be dealt with."
- "I had too many phone calls or emails to return."
- "Another matter was more important."
- "Traffic was bad."
- "I was in another meeting that ran too long."

The reality is that every time you are late you damage your personal brand and hurt your organization. Be responsible when making commitments and try to keep them. People would not invite you unless they felt it was important for you to be there to give your input. If you do not want to participate in a meeting, do not accept the invitation. If you are in the habit of overcommitting yourself . . . stop!

Overcommitting is not helpful to anyone, including you. If you question the value of a meeting, or your need to be there, do so beforehand. Most importantly, be respectful to everyone. Leaders who have the mindset that "I am the boss so everyone else should wait" are usually the ones who have the lowest employee engagement and productivity.

Measuring the Success of a Meeting

Do you measure the success of a meeting by whether it started or ended on time or that you completed your agenda? Many times meetings do both but accomplish nothing. I suggest changing the measurement system.

If you are leading a business and see your job as working *on* a business rather than *in* it, then expect to attend lots of meetings. Leaders should get over the number and length of meetings they attend and instead concern themselves with the quality and success of those meetings. Most organizations are not having too many meetings. They are having too many bad meetings.

Measure the effectiveness of your meetings. As I mentioned earlier, a good leading indicator that something important is being discussed are the different opinions in the room—conflict—and that most of the people are engaged in the discussion. Other indicators of good meetings are the number of critical decisions made, new actions developed, the number of new ideas created and accepted, and the increase in percentage of goals achieved. If you have a really good meeting, everyone leaves feeling invested in the decisions that were made and aligned as a team!

Selecting Your Attendees Properly

How do you decide who will participate in a particular meeting? Just because someone has a specific title or is part of a work group does not entitle or require that person to be in your meeting. The key considerations for inclusion are: purpose, contribution, influence, developmental factors, and productivity.

The most important factor when deciding who to include in your meetings is the purpose of your meeting. By focusing on just a few topics, you can limit attendees to only those people who are likely to have significant influence or input on the addressed topics. In that way, you maximize the productivity and value that come from your meeting. For example, if the meeting's purpose is to make a decision on a particular topic, it will be important to have all of the decision makers and influencers in the room. Failure to do so would result in fragmenting the discussion and delaying the decision.

Other factors to consider regarding contribution and influence include: subject matter expertise, functional expertise, and the willingness and authority to act. You want to invite people from inside and outside your organization who bring the most value in terms of subject matter expertise. Too often I see leaders making decisions based on belief rather than knowledge. In addition, they leave out critical functional expertise such as information technology, human resources, and finance. Often these functions are left out of strategic and operational discussions on the front end. The consequences of these omissions can be fragmented processes and systems, cost overruns, delays in product launches, cultural breakdowns, etc.

Another factor to consider is the development of the team. For your organization to grow, your people need to grow. Including people from different levels in the same meeting promotes everyone's growth. While the lower-level people may contribute less in the meetings, they have a chance to learn from participating. It also gives you and the other leaders a chance to transmit your company's DNA to a broader audience. In addition to increasing the size of your meetings slightly to include "high-potentials," you may want to consider a rotation program that gives everyone exposure to your meetings over the course of the year. This gives you the benefit of helping them grow, and you may be surprised by their input.

Two other important stakeholders often excluded from meetings are the people who need to execute your ideas and decisions and the people who will block them. In the former group are the frontline people who really have a sense of what it takes to get things done. Too often, leaders are big-picture people who may have subject-matter expertise but have lost touch (if they ever had it) with what it really takes to make things happen. In addition, they underestimate the detractors and do not consider the people aspects of driving change in their organization. We not only need the thinkers and deciders in the room, we also need some doers.

Avoid These Three Common Meeting Pitfalls
Now that we have discussed exactly how to create strong and well-considered meetings, let's shift to some of the biggest mistakes people make during these meetings. I have isolated three of the most common pitfalls to help you identify whether they apply to your meetings.

1. *Are you potentially seeing your role in the wrong way?*
    The most serious meeting participation pitfall is the leader who wants to give the answers to everyone in the room. Don't get me wrong here; sometimes the team needs answers from the senior leader. However, great leaders understand their role in meetings: Ask the right questions and access the ideas of their team. They realize there are many ways to do things. So they put big ideas on the table, ask difficult questions, and

get the team to debate those ideas. Once they've listened to everyone's points of view, they then combine that input with their own ideas and make the best decisions possible. The leader's job is to access the brains of the team, not to be the brain.

2. *Do you have a tendency to jump into problem-solving mode too quickly?*
Another common mistake I see in meetings is the tendency to jump too quickly into problem-solving mode. As soon as a meeting participant raises an issue, concern, or problem, everyone moves too quickly to find a solution or provide an answer. The value of having multiple people available is to first determine whether you're addressing a symptom or the real problem. The greatest value participants bring to a meeting is to ask great questions. It is common for a presenter to consciously or unconsciously omit important information the other participants need to know. Once these facts are uncovered by the questions being asked, you may find there is a more fundamental or broader issue to solve than the original symptom mentioned at the onset.

3. *Is everyone's contribution being heard?*
The leader of a meeting must ensure the whole team gets involved in the discussions. Some additional dimensions to this issue are:

   a. <u>Failure to voice your opinions, questions, and concerns</u>: If you do not contribute, you have wasted your time and everyone else's. Everyone has something to contribute. Failure to speak up begs the question "Why are you here to begin with?" Leaders must recognize the people in the room who have lower self-confidence and tend to defer to others and must make sure they are accessing their brainpower. For many people, failure to speak does not mean they do not have a lot of value to bring. It is your job to make sure you get it.

   b. <u>Overcontributors</u>: Have you ever attended a meeting where one person in the room has to have their opinion heard on every point? They monopolize all the talk time! A good leader will make sure others have a chance to speak and limit the amount of time they give to the overcontributor.

c. <u>Active Listening</u>: Identify what is *not* being said. Watching people's body language, listening to tone, and understanding why they say what they say is many times more important than the words they say. Ninety-three percent of communication is not the words people use. A good leader actively listens during the meeting. This helps to ensure that when decisions are made and plans are set, everyone is committed.

Creating a positive, well-developed strategy for meetings will ensure you don't permit a ton of unnecessary leaks within your bucket.

Key Chapter Points:
Profit Leak #14: *Ineffective Meetings or Lack of Meetings*

- Well-executed meetings can accelerate and improve the decision-making process, align the team, improve prioritization, and make communication more efficient. When done poorly, meetings do none of these things.
- Status updates are not a great use of time and should take up no more than 15 percent of your meetings.
- We examined eight factors that can improve your meetings:
  1. Constructive conflict
     - A strong leading indicator of a great meeting is when something important is discussed and improved upon via opinions and conflict. It is a bad sign when you are the only one considering the options for an important decision.
     - A good meeting increases your options in making a decision.
     - A proper meeting environment allows everyone to do their best thinking.
  2. Focus on purpose rather than agendas
     - Focus your meetings around decisions and the nature of the decisions.
  3. Set aside enough time to achieve your purpose

- Failure to debate priorities and work through issues can bring organizations to a standstill while leaders wait until the next meeting for a final decision, allowing your competition the opportunity to thrust forward.

4. Establish proper meeting rhythms

   - Highly effective organizations have learned to schedule a good series of daily "huddles" and weekly, monthly, quarterly, and annual meetings can be carefully designed to get all of the right people together at the same time.

   - Each meeting is assigned a purpose built around specific decisions to be made.

5. Start meetings on time and keep commitments

   - Every time you are late you damage your personal brand and hurt your organization.

   - Overcommitting is not helpful to anyone, including yourself.

   - If you question the value of a meeting, or your need to be there, do so beforehand.

6. Measure the success of each meeting based on:

   - Number of critical decisions made

   - Number of new actions developed

   - Number of new ideas created and accepted

   - Investment of team in a decision

7. Select your attendees properly.

8. Avoid the three most common meeting pitfalls:

   - Know your role.

   - Everyone should contribute and not overcontribute.

   - Actively listen.

---- Chapter 19 ----

PROFIT LEAK #15
Failing to Create a Culture of Accountability

W e just discussed the importance of communication, meetings, and goal setting. Your ultimate desire should be to create a culture that supports these crucial pillars. To do so, ensure that you and your team are accountable. Have you ever wondered why so many annual plans fail? Has your organization ever failed to achieve key priorities in your own plan? Many leaders claim they've achieved their results but are often unwilling or unable to show you exactly how. Only a company with great execution would be proud to open their doors to the public and allow others to take a look behind the curtains. Leaders who have done so know it isn't likely that someone could ever copy their accomplishments. They have the secret sauce and know you can taste it but not steal it. Great execution is the equivalent of a harmonious symphony with a thousand instruments playing at once. It takes hard work and discipline to pull it off. Moreover, if you place any successful company under a microscope, you're likely to find that accountability plays an enormous role in its accomplishments.

Accountability is a culture, process, and systems component that spans the organizational spectrum. In general, most employees do not think their company holds all team members equally accountable for their responsibilities and actions. They are not wrong. Accountability is typically found to be weak among partners, owners, and executive teams, usually because these groups allow relationships to take precedence over the best interests of the organization.

By and large, accountability processes and systems exist. However, they often lack depth and do not work properly. In many cases, leadership does not enforce policies that were designed to hold others responsible. For example, the most effective way to hold salespeople accountable is to measure the daily activities that lead to sales, yet many companies experience tremendous difficulty in enforcing adequate usage of the Customer Relationship Management system. Experience has proven that when compliance is truly mandatory, salespeople provide the data, and management and salespeople find useful data that leads to a more productive sales organization. Failure to do so makes most companies miss a lot of opportunities.

To address accountability in your organization, I suggest you examine these five aspects in your operations:

1. Maintaining the right level of conflict
2. Establishing personal priorities that are aligned to company priorities
3. Implementing action plans for each priority
4. Sending clear messages
5. Monitoring progress and having a continuous feedback loop

Let's examine each of these more closely.

Conflict Is Necessary for Success

Expect and encourage constructive conflict to help accomplish anything of consequence in your company. Constructive conflict means welcoming differences of opinion about strategies and tactics that stay within the bounds of civility. Conflict is a necessity when developing your priorities or addressing accountability. Conflict often leads to better resolutions, as it requires numerous opinions and feedback to crystallize your objectives. Failure to have conflict leaves some people feeling unheard and allows other people to get off the hook. It will spell trouble in the long run. To achieve true consensus and stick to deadlines, make sure you hear your team out and do not allow excuses when they fail to deliver. Everyone should feel invested in decisions so they will be accountable and aligned as a team!

Start by questioning your culture if your team does not speak up when new decisions are being made or when they fail to follow through. For example, leaders often state they want others' opinions, but their actions say otherwise. There should be good, healthy conflict, particularly when setting company priorities, and people should venture out of their comfort zones. Your team should agree on what will and will *not* get done.

Do not confuse conflict and debate with simply creating stress for your team. Some leaders do not know the difference. Make sure your discussions occur in an environment where everyone is stretched and able to do their best thinking. As mentioned earlier, lack of conflict or engaged dialogue among the team indicates you are not talking about anything that requires any real discussion, you are failing to emphasize the hard-to-achieve goals and key performance indicators, not holding people accountable, or not discussing the elephants in the room. The lack of conflict can also be an indication that the foundation of a strong team—trust—is missing. Once decisions are made, your team must drive those decisions home, still allowing for natural conflict to occur.

Personal Priorities Must Support Organizational Priorities

While few companies have quarterly plans that align with their annual plans, even fewer have personal quarterly plans that align leaders with the company quarterly plans. So it is not surprising that a company can create quarterly goals and priorities and then fall short of actually executing the plans. Setting company priorities is just the beginning. Another key distinguishing factor of the One-Page Strategic Plan referred to in an earlier chapter is that every leader on the team is required to develop their own *personal* quarterly plan that aligns with the company's plan. Personal quarterly plans include the goals, key performance indicators, Critical Numbers, and three to five personal priorities each leader will strive to achieve.

Accountability is best served when you assign specific tasks to individual team members. Some unlucky person may get more than one and have to prioritize which tasks are the most important to achieving the company's overall goals. Leaders can help with that, offering team members specific guidelines to accomplish these newly assigned responsibilities. Each leader considers his or her function or role in the company and understands how he or she can make the biggest impact in elevating it. Leaders also consider the company's quarterly priorities and annual initiatives and goals to determine how their actions can either be accelerators or bottlenecks to success. Inspiring each department to improve the right Critical Number each quarter will continue to elevate each leader and enable your company to reach peak performance.

Action Plans Will Keep You on Track

After conducting more than a thousand business planning sessions and reviewing results with leadership teams, I've found that a well-conceptualized action plan is a common thread in the successful ones. The majority of companies without an action plan failed, while those with a strong action plan reached their goals approximately 75 percent of the time. Additionally, even in the cases where there was a failed action plan, businesses made substantial progress on their prioritization process. Action plans are critical to your success, so much so that I can easily outline some of the most valuable results of a strong action plan. These include:

1. Create a framework for accountability.
2. Clarify responsibility.
3. Help identify obstacles to success.
4. Crystallize and align agreement around the path to getting things done.
5. Provide deadlines.
6. Foster commitment.
7. Develop mechanisms to warn you when you are off course.

I feel comfortable that you'd agree each of these will not only impact the overall success, but also the bottom line of your business. Who wouldn't want to create clarity with, and commitment from, their team? Work hard to establish a strong action plan to ensure your team remains on track and moving in the right direction.

Are You Sending Mixed Messages?

Creating quarterly plans, personal plans, and action plans positions you for excellence, but you still have to send the right messages to your team. Often leadership teams are full of people who like to chase shiny objects. The brightest shiny object is usually instant gratification in some form—today's sale, a specific customer problem, general employee concerns, or any number of other immediate, non-crucial issues. Think of the rocks exercise. Getting caught up in the day-to-day can cause you to lose sight of the long game.

You can afford to be nimble when you are a small company with few employees. It doesn't take much energy or effort to rapidly change your priorities. In fact, all of these steps I referenced can be done on the fly. However, the more employees you have, the costlier and more difficult it becomes to zig and zag. To do so, make your processes consistent, define employees' roles, and create definitive plans. You have to provide your team with clear marching orders and the confidence to know they are going to stick. Few things are more frustrating than starting and stopping projects because of a lack of discipline. It destroys motivation and employee engagement. After a while your team members will not respect your initiatives. They will wait to start projects to confirm you are serious and will not suddenly change course. You then lose time and money because of a lack of trust.

Failing to follow through on stated initiatives happens all of the time, especially when your company fails to create a culture of accountability. A great example is a Chief Operations Officer (COO) I encountered who had accountability for everything, authority for nothing, and was left responsible for everything. Here are some examples of what this person's role looked like:

- If anything went wrong in the company, the COO was faulted for not having a process in place to prevent it from day one.
- The COO led approximately 50 employees and was expected to know what each employee had accomplished on any given day.
- Salespeople were supposed to be left to their own devices, so long as they caused no issues that impacted overall goals. When they did, it was the fault of the COO.
- Knowing it would be the fault of the COO if anything went wrong empowered the salespeople to make unachievable promises to customers.
- The Chief Executive Officer (CEO) protected employees based solely on their relationship with him, regardless of their job performance. If they did not do their jobs, the COO was expected to step in and do it for them.

In this COO example, the CEO indicated he wanted only the best possible people on the company team and everyone held accountable for their performance. He said he wanted the COO to succeed. The CEO then created an environment that set the COO up for mission impossible and certain failure.

Create a Culture of Accountability

Employees are destined for failure if they do not have a clear plan of action, goals to work toward, and Critical Numbers by which to measure their accomplishments. How else could you hold them accountable? A goal or Critical Number without an action plan is nothing more than a hope or a dream. In addition, responsibility and accountability are too often given without authority to accomplish the work. You have to work to set your people up for success. Once you are comfortable with their action plans, start to delegate sufficient authority so they can move quickly and without restriction. Then you need to measure the results of their tasks. Measurement is at the center of accountability.

Start by creating a central place where your team can see progress toward your plans, goals, and Critical Numbers. This information should be updated in daily, weekly, and monthly increments. Most importantly, discuss progress.

If people know you are watching, their basic human nature will accelerate their progress.

An example of this is what I can accomplish thanks to the data provided to me by the county public school system. I receive a daily email informing me of whether my children attended their classes, as well as their grades. If either has an unexcused absence or something unexpected happens with their grades, I can launch an immediate dialogue to address the issue. Of course, I do not like having to do that, nor do they like the fact I do it. However, my kids have never had an unexplained absence and can immediately work toward improving their grades. They are aware of this accountability program, and it forces them to make the right decisions, or face immediate feedback.

The same needs to happen with your key business information. Find the leading indicators that allow you to have discussions with team members, increase and change resources when necessary, and make key decisions to ensure you perform at peak levels. Define action plans weekly so you can keep team members on track. Focus on Critical Numbers in your daily huddles. In weekly meetings, review your dashboards to ensure your key numbers are at acceptable levels. By the time you reach a monthly meeting, you can have broader conversations and midcourse corrections to handle any huge and unforeseen obstacles.

You may be saying, "Do I really have to do this? I hired capable people, so I can trust them to do their job." The answer: Yes, you have to do this—you have to create a process and system to ensure everyone is on the same page. Create a simple process to confirm everyone is focused on the right things and that you do not lose track of short-term and long-term goals. It is too easy to get sucked into the day-to-day chaos and forget where you were headed in the first place. This is the essential reason accountability is one of the biggest issues in most organizations.

Help your team members create a specific roadmap to success by:

- Aligning your incentives with strategic objectives.
- Increasing your focus in the organization around the activities that have the biggest positive impact.

- Communicating your goals and objectives to everyone in the organization.
- Ensuring there is only one person accountable for each initiative, process, and desired outcome.

Key Chapter Points

Profit Leak #15: *Failing to Create a Culture of Accountability*

- Accountability is a culture, process, and systems component that spans the organizational spectrum.
- Leadership must enforce policy related to tools that were designed to hold others responsible or the tools and policies will not work.
- Expect and encourage constructive conflict to help accomplish anything of consequence in your company.
    - Constructive conflict means differences of opinion about strategies and tactics that stay within the bounds of civility.
    - Conflict often leads to the best resolutions, as it requires numerous opinions and feedback to crystallize your objectives.
    - Failure to have conflict leaves some people feeling unheard and allows other people to get off the hook.
    - Do not confuse conflict and debate with simply creating stress for your team.
- Personal plans that are aligned to the company's quarterly plan are essential to quarterly success.
- A well-conceptualized action plan is a common thread in those who are successful.
    - The majority of companies without an action plan failed, while those with a strong action plan reached their goals approximately 75 percent of the time.
    - Seven reasons why action plans are critical to your success:
        1. Create a framework for accountability
        2. Clarify responsibility
        3. Help identify obstacles to success

4. Crystallize and align agreement around the path to getting things done

5. Provide deadlines

6. Foster commitment

7. Develop mechanisms to warn you when you are off course

- Be careful not to send mixed messages about what your priorities are.
- Create an environment that fosters a culture of accountability.

PART V
PLUGGING THE HOLES
IN THE BUCKET

"Rarely do we find men who willingly engage in hard, solid thinking. There is an almost universal quest for easy answers and half-baked solutions. Nothing pains some people more than having to think."
—**Martin Luther King Jr.**[64]

Chapter 20

STOPPING THE LEAKS

A t this point, you should feel better equipped to recognize and understand the potential leaks any business may face. Businesses are always at risk, and even the leanest and best-run organizations can, and do, leak away valuable time and resources if their c-suite executives and team members do not maintain vigilance. Throughout this book we have examined 15 specific leaks that often latch onto businesses and create large holes in their buckets. To refresh your memory, these include:

People Leaks

Profit Leak #1: *Poor Leadership*

Profit Leak #2: *"B" and "C" Players*

Profit Leak #3: *Financial Transparency*

Profit Leak #4: *Vacant Positions*

Profit Leak #5: *Excessive Turnover*

<u>**Strategy Leaks**</u>

Profit Leak #6: *Action Without Purpose*

Profit Leak #7: *Failing to Differentiate Properly*

Profit Leak #8: *Focusing on Tactics Instead of Strategy*

Profit Leak #9: *Chasing Revenue Everywhere and Anywhere*

<u>**Execution Leaks**</u>

Profit Leak #10: *Ineffectively Communicating Your Goals and Expectations*

Profit Leak #11: *Emphasizing the Wrong Priorities and Not Aligning the Team*

Profit Leak #12: *Being Allergic to Saying "No"*

Profit Leak #13: *Monitoring the Wrong Numbers*

Profit Leak #14: *Ineffective Meetings or Lack of Meetings*

Profit Leak #15: *Failing to Create a Culture of Accountability*

While this is not an all-encompassing list, it does outline the most substantial and common leaks your company may encounter. Start by reviewing this list, then ask yourself: "Which of these list items apply to me?" If you circle one, or even more than one, it is time to consider implementing changes to prevent any further loss of time, money, or other valuable resources.

Every strong business dedicated to continued growth and development is willing to first evaluate its present circumstances. Next, it analyzes where it can improve. Finally, it implements a plan to address these issues. As you progress through this process, recognize the numerous resources at your disposal.

If you have read this all the way through, you may be feeling excited and overwhelmed. You are excited about the number of opportunities available to help you improve your business. At the same time, if you are being honest, you are somewhat overwhelmed by the amount of work you think needs to be done before you can capture all the money your team is potentially leaving on the table. It is natural for you to wonder exactly where you can start.

There are proven approaches to identifying and prioritizing your leaks. This is where a coach can help! Most times it is easier for a third party to help you see the right actions to be taken. They are not invested in the issues or the outcomes. The coach can bring a new perspective to your leaks by asking unbiased questions.

They are persistent and ask the right questions to ensure you do not misdiagnose a situation. Coaches are catalysts that can facilitate discussion between leaders to drive proper accountability.

Also, you may be thinking, *Can I do this without outside help?* This is a fair question. You know your business better than anyone, but sometimes you cannot see the forest for the trees. The fact is, you already know you could have gotten better results, but did not. You could have implemented certain practices and did not. Even if you have effected some change on your own, why would you not want to get the best results possible?

To master the concepts in this book, I recommend that every leader take two steps:

1. The first is to get a coach.
2. The second is to implement and master a "Leadership Operating System" (LOS).[65]

Step One: Get a Coach

Let's first tackle the topic of choosing a coach. I have hired a number of coaches over my lifetime and am certain there will be more. The main reason is well documented in the *Fast Company* magazine article "Dismantling the Myth of the Self-Reliant CEO," written by Allen Gannett. In the article he describes how leaders obtain and choose their professional support system.

Gannett found that more and more CEOs are joining support groups like YPO, Vistage, and EO for peer mentoring. In fact, they are more likely to get a coach as the company scales. They are not the bulletproof superheroes they appear to be from the outside. You may find it interesting that the serial CEOs and growing companies are the ones that often seek the most help. You would think it would be the opposite, but the best are always seeking the most support. According to the data, 60% of growth-stage CEOs sought help from executive coaches while only 32% of early-stage CEOs did the same. Executive coaching employs methods such as asking the important questions to gain insight from your own assumptions. It is a delicate process that provides a more direct and personal angle to arrive at a self-initiated meaningful action and outcome.[66]

The process of business coaching addresses the long-term questions and possible results to help you understand how your decisions contribute to the current business standing.

An executive coach understands the urgency and calls of the modern business landscape. That's why it's also important for us to share the necessary skills in real time within the context of the urgent issues and challenges you need to address. They make it a point to provide you with a broader take on identifying and tackling problems, working them out strategically, and applying the right kind of solutions. You can expect that after all the plans are laid out, you can review them and carefully consider the best course of action—because you're always the best person to make the call.

A coach functions as an external consultation partner and not part of the company. His or her job is to guide you through the process of generating a new outlook toward the business so you can think clearly, make the tough decisions, and avoid repeating bad patterns. Coaches are usually professionals who are experts in the field of business acceleration and improvisation. Throughout your relationship, expect to receive encouragement whenever you need it and full transparency.

Executive coaching helps you develop and hone your skills in "real time," within the context of the issues and challenges you want to address. While all forms of self-development and improvement are advantageous, executive coaching is more practical and effective than books, seminars, and improvement programs because it integrates teaching and insights into your life on a daily basis.

Rather than starting and stopping (like reading self-improvement books) or trying to cram all of your self-improvement into one small time frame outside the norm of your life (like attending a seminar), the benefits of executive coaching become an integral part of your life—the life you envisioned—as your dreams begin to become reality. Your self-esteem and confidence begin to soar as you start to realize more of your potential than even you thought possible!

An executive coach can help you understand your circumstances from various perspectives, learn new approaches, break bad habits, and challenge you to develop better strategies. Your coach can help you see how to move your skills forward, find blind spots, and learn how to become a more effective leader.

Here are some of the most noticeable benefits leaders just like YOU have experienced from working with the right executive coach:

- Heightened ability to influence others
- Improved performance and increased effectiveness
- Higher levels of self-confidence
- Increased self-awareness
- Challenge and support—the extra push when you need it
- Increased employee engagement
- Improved relationships at home and at work

Step Two: Implement and Master a "Leadership Operating System"

The second step: Implement a Leadership Operating System (LOS) that will help you seek out, identify, prioritize and address your Leaky Bucket. If your company is like most, at least 60 percent of the leaks identified in this book are issues you face. So you need a LOS to help you get your arms around this.

The LOS will begin with meeting rhythms. Construct the right set of meetings that involves everyone in your company so that information flows properly on a daily, weekly, and monthly basis. This allows the right decisions to be made faster at the right level in your company and for customers to be better served. One thing we have experienced over the last five years and can expect over the next five to ten years, thanks to technology, is that customers will expect faster service and communications and will not pay for it. Your organization needs to respond to this.

Your LOS and meeting rhythms should include proper time for strategy. Most leaders are spending far too little time on strategy and the underlying tactics. Strategy is not focusing on the current year. I recommend at least one day per quarter. Most leaders need help learning how to talk about strategy and need a framework. Given the speed at which the world is changing, your strategy will need to change more frequently than it has in the past. If you look at the Fortune 500 list of largest public companies, the rate of extinction has gone from 67 years to 15 years. Comparing the Fortune 500 companies in 1955 to the Fortune 500 in 2014, only 61 still exist and 88 percent are gone.[67]

Your LOS and meeting rhythms must align on priorities. Too often organizations have been planning processes where they set goals and initiatives and the organization does something else. This is usually the result of a weak LOS. While priorities need to change sometimes, this should be the exception rather than the rule. Make sure the big things get done and many of your smaller issues go away.

Your LOS must have an organization of people living shared values focused on customers. The leadership paradigm where leaders hoard all the information, need to make all the decisions, and tell everyone else what to do does not work in today's business world. You need an operating system that creates an environment where employees enjoy working for your company and are empowered to take action. The employees know what is expected of them and can act off script because their positions require people who can think and act on changing information.

A LOS I use and have alluded to throughout this book, *Four Decisions*™, based on Harnish's *Scaling Up*, leverages concepts derived from the works of best-selling authors and addresses areas of people, strategy, execution, and cash. You can derive the best results when implemented in conjunction with an ongoing coaching relationship. The coaching relationship fosters stronger accountability and with the right coach can be directed toward accelerating your business performance. The process helps you define and align your long-term strategy, annual business plan, quarterly plan, and individual priorities to grow a better business.

How much potential for growth do you leave on the table each month? The right business coach likely has the 10,000+ hours of practice necessary to help companies like yours implement programs that work and can accelerate the process. Every passing week and month can result in significant terms of growth, cash, and stress that you can never recover once you have lost them.

I share all of this because I wrote this book to help you and your business gain access to the knowledge, tools, and resources necessary to maximize your success. I want to encourage you to read *Scaling Up*, and if you decide to hire a coach, *Scaling Up* will give you a website that identifies other coaches like me. There are approximately 150 coaches worldwide at this time. I am honored to have a mastermind group that includes eight other highly skilled business coaches from around the US and Canada. We are some of the most senior and experienced coaches in implementing the *Scaling Up* tools, and I would gladly introduce you to any of them. I am proud to have them as colleagues and to be a member of the same think tank.

Your company's issues might resemble those of some of my clients who were highly successful from all outward appearances. Prior to working with coaches and having the right LOS, they already had the unusual value proposition, consistent organic growth rates in revenue and profits, exceeded their competition, and realized profit margins were above the norm. In many cases I even had the pleasure to find a great team running the show. However, my clients will also tell you they were thankful for the tools, experience, and veracity I brought to the table. Many had imminent danger they could not see, were complacent and did not realize it, and had big profit leaks sitting right before their eyes. It was much easier for an outsider like me to see the bigger picture.

For example, one CEO I have been working with for the last three years has grown quite a bit. He has been the envy of his peers in Entrepreneur's Organization for the way he has grown a profitable company at such a young age, especially without the need for external capital. His company is global. He is in the technology industry, has been profitable since the beginning, and his company grows at more than 20 percent annually. However, through our work together, he uncovered blind spots in how he assembled and built his team, measured success, and approached his innovation process. Our discussions recently uncovered some bottlenecks in the growth of his core business as well as some real imminent danger in the future viability of the company. We addressed those issues, made adjustments, and ensured he is again humming along.

On the other hand, you may resemble another client whose business was at the other extreme. In the first 90 days of our work together, we were able to take a business that generated negative cash flow on approximately $10 million in revenue and turn that into $600,000 in positive cash flow. We did this with adjustments, not the need for additional growth. Shockingly, the owners had not realized they had generated negative cash flow for the full calendar year prior to beginning our work together. We quickly identified team members who were sitting in the wrong seats and others who could not perform at the required levels. By focusing on five key priorities and making a few key staff changes, they are positioning themselves to have a much more successful business.

The question to ask at this point is this: *Is now the right time?*

Leaders like to say they "don't have time" to work with a coach or to implement the ideas suggested in this book. It is common for them to believe there will be a better time in some distant future—once they've changed a few key people, completed that big transaction, finished a big project, or arrived at some other natural business crossroads. In reality, when was the last time you thought you had plenty of extra time on your hands? The answer is probably never, and if you did, you were in denial.

The right time is now! You can get better results from activities you are already doing today. A business coach can help you reallocate how you go about doing your activities. In the long run we help YOU find more time, by helping YOU figure out how you are wasting time, how YOU can work less, and how YOU can get a better result from time worked.

And then you may ask this: *Will the process be right for my business?*

I often hear the question "What if this process does not work?" Business coaching is different from consulting. As long as you hire a business coach who is bringing in proven business operating processes, your concern about it working is the equivalent of saying, "What if I inhale and air does not fill my lungs?" In short, the process will provide the results. In my experience, the steps succeed to the degree that you commit to the work and do it. Not doing the work means you're willing to allow the Leaky Bucket to continue leaking every day. Everything we offer as a business team has already been proven in thousands of companies to close your leaks and help you prosper. They are the business fundamentals that everyone knows, but many don't do.

Are you ready?

Are you ready to change?

Are you willing to grow?

Are you excited to develop?

The answer to all of these very simple questions should be an emphatic "YES!" Get a coach and implement a proven LOS. I am confident you'll find opportunities to recognize the leaks and then plug them. Henry Ford said, "Coming together is a beginning; keeping together is progress; working together is success."[68] Through this book, we have come together. If you have made it this far, we have remained together. And now, I am excited to work with you to help you recognize the leaks, plug the bucket, and build the business of your dreams.

REFERENCES

1   "Shigeo Shingo Quotes," As of 9/15/2016, http://www.azquotes.com/
author/44596-Shigeo_Shingo.

2   Jim Collins, *Good to Great: Why Companies Make the Leap...and Others
Don't* (HarperCollins Publishers, 2001), 41-64.

3   Alina Dizik, *Career Advice from Iconic Leaders*, April 4, 2011, CNN
Website Living Section, http://www.cnn.com/2011/LIVING/04/04/
cb.world.leader.career.tips/.

4   "Albert Einstein Quotes." AZQuotes, As of 9/15/2016, http://www.
azquotes.com/quote/360150

5   Gallup, Inc., *State of the American Workplace: Employee Engagement Insights
for U.S. Business Leaders*, Research Report, 2013, 19.

6   Quotes Falsely Attributed to Winston Churchill, As of 9/15/2016, http://
www.winstonchurchill.org/resources/quotations/135-quotes-falsely-
attributed

7   Verne Harnish, *Scaling Up: How Few Companies Make It...and the Rest
Don't* (Gazelles, Inc., 2014), 85.

8   Leonard Pitts, "Why Politics Has Become So Destructive," *Miami Herald*,
February 1, 2009, L1

9   Bradford D. Smart Ph. D, *Topgrading, 3rd Edition: The Proven Hiring and Promoting Method That Turbocharges Company Performance,* (Penguin, 2012), 28.

10 Verne Harnish, *Scaling Up: How Few Companies Make It…and the Rest Don't* (Gazelles, Inc., 2014), 70-71.

11 Michael Jordan's Unofficial Guide to Success in the NBA, Bleacher Report, Dan Favale, Feb 14, 2013, http://bleacherreport.com/articles/1529861-michael-jordans-unofficial-guide-to-success-in-the-nba.

12 Alan Miltz, "Cash Flow is King" (presentation to Gazelles International Coaches about the Cash Flow Story model and philosophy, GI Coaches Summit, Las Vegas, NV, October 27, 2014).

13 Verne Harnish, *Scaling Up: How Few Companies Make It…and the Rest Don't* (Gazelles, Inc., 2014), 15-17.

14 The 25 Smartest Things Warren Buffett Ever Said, The Motley Fool, February 26, 2012, http://www.fool.com.au/2012/02/26/the-25-smartest-things-warren-buffett-ever-said/

15 Bob Hill, "Apple CEO Steve Jobs' '12 Rules of Success'," BusinessBrief.com, September, 9, 2009, http://www.businessbrief.com/apple-ceo-steve-jobs-12-rules-of-success/.

16 Gallop, Inc., *State of the American Workplace: Employee Engagement Insights for U.S. Business Leaders*, Research Report, 2013, 9-21.

17 Jim Loehr, *The Only Way to Win: How Building Character Drives Higher Achievement and Greater Fulfillment in Business and Life* (Hachette Book Group, 2012), 43-73.

18 Jim Loehr, *The Only Way to Win: How Building Character Drives Higher Achievement and Greater Fulfillment in Business and Life* (Hachette Book Group, 2012), 43-73.

19 General Stanley McChrystal et al, Team of Teams: New Rules of Engagement for a Complex World (Penguin 2015), 220-226.

20 Bradford D. Smart Ph. D, *Topgrading, 3rd Edition: The Proven Hiring and Promoting Method That Turbocharges Company Performance,* (Penguin, 2012), 24-52.

21 Kip Tindell, "Uncontainable" (presentation about his new book regard the keys to his organization's success from start-up to present, Fortune Growth Summit, Dallas, Texas, October 20, 2015).

22 What Gets Measured Gets Done, Tom Peters, As of 9/16/2016, http://tompeters.com/columns/what-gets-measured-gets-done/.

23 Why Most Venture Backed Companies Fail, Fast Company Website by Faisal Hoque, December 10, 12, https://www.fastcompany.com/3003827/why-most-venture-backed-companies-fail.

24 Alan Miltz, "Cash Flow is King" (presentation to Gazelles International Coaches about the Cash Flow Story model and philosophy, GI Coaches Summit, Las Vegas, NV, October 27, 2014).

25 Bradford D. Smart Ph. D, *Topgrading, 3*rd *Edition: The Proven Hiring and Promoting Method That Turbocharges Company Performance*, (Penguin, 2012), 66.

26 Bradford D. Smart Ph. D, *Topgrading, 3*rd *Edition: The Proven Hiring and Promoting Method That Turbocharges Company Performance*, (Penguin, 2012), 66.

27 Verne Harnish, *Scaling Up: How Few Companies Make It...and the Rest Don't* (Gazelles, Inc., 2014), 42-43.

28 Verne Harnish, *Scaling Up: How Few Companies Make It...and the Rest Don't* (Gazelles, Inc., 2014), 46-57.

29 Kip Tindell, "Uncontainable" (presentation about his new book regard the keys to his organization's success from start-up to present, Fortune Growth Summit, Dallas, Texas, October 20, 2015).

30 Tammy Erickson, "The Biggest Mistakes You (Probably) Make with Teams," Harvard Business Review. April 5, 2012, Tammy Erickson, https://hbr.org/2012/04/the-biggest-mistake-you-probab

31 Bradford D. Smart Ph. D, *Topgrading, 3*rd *Edition: The Proven Hiring and Promoting Method That Turbocharges Company Performance*, (Penguin, 2012), 53-179

32 Adam Vaccaro, "Why Employees Quit Jobs Right After They've Started," Inc., April 17, 2014, http://www.inc.com/adam-vaccaro/voluntary-turnover-six-months.html

33 Executive Coaching Yields Return of Almost Six Times its Cost!, Work / Life Solutions, Inc., 1/04/2001, file:///C:/Users/howard/Downloads/ManchesterExecutiveCoachingYieldsWorkLifeSoluti%20(1).pdf.

34 Return on Investment, Performance Coaching International, As of 9/17/2016, http://www.performancecoachinginternational.com/resources/roi.php.

35 The Churchill Centre, As of 9/17/2016, http://www.winstonchurchill.org/support?catid=0&id=1648.

36 Verne Harnish, *Scaling Up: How Few Companies Make It...and the Rest Don't* (Gazelles, Inc., 2014).

37 How to Act from Purpose: Ask and Listen, Huffington Post, February 11, 2014, http://www.huffingtonpost.com/cortney-mcdermott/how-to-act-from-purpose-a_b_4428355.html.

38 Gazelles International Growth Workshop, Slide Deck, Strategy Section, As of September 17, 2016.

39 BrainyQuote, as of September 17, 2016, http://www.brainyquote.com/quotes/quotes/a/alberteins385842.html.

40 Top 15 Most Popular Search Engines, eBiz/MBA, As of September 1, 2016, http://www.ebizmba.com/articles/search-engines.

41 Apple, Google Top The World's Most Valuable Brands Of 2016, Kurt Badenhausen, May 11, 2016, http://www.forbes.com/sites/kurtbadenhausen/2016/05/11/the-worlds-most-valuable-brands/#47b49e7a7561.

42 Study: Many Searchers Choose Google Over Bing Even When Google's Name Is On Bing's Results, Search Engine Land, Amy Gesenhues, April 15, 2013, http://searchengineland.com/users-prefer-google-even-when-155682.

43 Alexander Osterwalder & Yves Pigneur, *Business Model Generation*, (Wiley 2010).

44 Sharon Terlep, "Unilever Buys Dollar Shave Club: European giant to pay $1 billion for startup in challenge to P&G," July 20, 2016, http://www.wsj.com/articles/unilever-buys-dollar-shave-club-1468987836.

45 Alexander Osterwalder & Yves Pigneur, *Business Model Generation*, (Wiley 2010), 22-25.

46 W. Chan Kim and Renée Mauborgne, *Blue Ocean Strategy*, (Harvard Review Press 2005).

47 Alexander Osterwalder & Yves Pigneur, *Business Model Generation*, (Wiley 2010).

48 Jim Collins, *Good to Great: Why Companies Make the Leap...and Others Don't* (HarperCollins Publishers, 2001), 114 -116.

49 Youngme Moon, "IKEA Invades America" (Case Study, Harvard Business School, 2004).

50 Steve Hedlund and Mark Schweitzer, "Reality Is Perception: The Truth about Car Brands, Evan Hirsh," Strategy + Business, Fall 2003, http://www.strategy-business.com/article/03302?gko=fbb50.

51 Gabriel Weinberg and Justin Mares, *Traction: How Any Startup Can Achieve Explosive Customer Growth*, (Portfolio, 2015).

52 Good Reads, As of September 17, 2016, http://www.goodreads.com/quotes/6862779-ideas-are-easy-it-s-the-execution-of-ideas-that-really.

53 Duncan Haughey, "SMART Goals," Project Smart, As of September 17, 2017, https://www.projectsmart.co.uk/smart-goals.php.

54 Don Clark, Visual, Auditory, and Kinesthetic Learning Styles (VAK), Big Dog, Little Dog and Knowledge Jump, As of September 17, 2016, http://www.nwlink.com/~donclark/hrd/styles/vakt.html.

55 Verne Harnish, *Scaling Up: How Few Companies Make It...and the Rest Don't* (Gazelles, Inc., 2014), 13-14, 86, 91-91, 107-108, 123-140, 150, 174, 177.

56 Verne Harnish, *Scaling Up: How Few Companies Make It...and the Rest Don't* (Gazelles, Inc., 2014), 13-14, 86, 91-91, 107-108, 123-140, 150, 174, 177.

57 First Things First, Dr. Stephen R. Covey, http://www.appleseeds.org/big-rocks_covey.htm.

58 Market Value of Selected Airlines Worldwide, Statista, As of July 2016, https://www.statista.com/statistics/275948/market-capitalization-of-selected-airlines/

59 Lisa D. Ordóñez et al, "Goals Gone Wild: The Systematic Side Effects of Over-Prescribing Goal Setting," Harvard Business School, Working Paper Summaries, February 11, 2009, http://hbswk.hbs.edu/item/goals-gone-wild-the-systematic-side-effects-of-over-prescribing-goal-setting.

60 Gazelles International Growth Workshop, Slide Deck, Execution Section, As of September 17, 2016.

61 Verne Harnish, *Scaling Up: How Few Companies Make It...and the Rest Don't* (Gazelles, Inc., 2014), 13-14, 86, 91-91, 107-108, 123-140, 150, 174, 177.

62 Patrick Lencioni, *Death by Meeting: A Leadership Fable...About Solving the Most Painful Problem in Business* (Jossey-Bass, 2004).

63 Verne Harnish, *Scaling Up: How Few Companies Make It...and the Rest Don't* (Gazelles, Inc., 2014), 9, 16, 175-190.

64 Martin Luther King Quotations, As of 09/19/2016, http://uspolitics. about.com/od/biographies/a/mlk_quotes.htm.

65 Gino Wickman, *Traction: Get a Grip on Your Business* (BenBella Books, April 2012).

66 Allen Gannett, "Dismantling the Myth of the Self-Reliant CEO, "Fast Company, May 26, 2016, https://www.fastcompany.com/3060235/dismantling-the-myth-of-the-self-reliant-ceo.

67 Mark J. Perry, "Fortune 500 firms in 1955 vs. 2014; 88% Are Gone, And We're All Better-off Because Of That Dynamic 'Creative Destruction'," AEI Business Ideas, August 18, 2014, https://www.aei.org/publication/fortune-500-firms-in-1955-vs-2014-89-are-gone-and-were-all-better-off-because-of-that-dynamic-creative-destruction/.

68 Coming Together Is a Beginning; Keeping Together Is Progress; Working Together Is Success., Forbes, Erika Andersen, May 31, 2013, http://www. forbes.com/sites/erikaandersen/2013/05/31/21-quotes-from-henry-ford-on-business-leadership-and-life/#6b31db473700.

A free eBook edition is available with the purchase of this book.

To claim your free eBook edition:

1. Download the Shelfie app.
2. Write your name in upper case in the box.
3. Use the Shelfie app to submit a photo.
4. Download your eBook to any device.

Shelfie

A free eBook edition is available
with the purchase of this print book.

CLEARLY PRINT YOUR NAME ABOVE IN UPPER CASE

Instructions to claim your free eBook edition:
1. Download the Shelfie app for Android or iOS
2. Write your name in **UPPER CASE** above
3. Use the Shelfie app to submit a photo
4. Download your eBook to any device

Print & Digital Together Forever.

Snap a photo

Free eBook

Read anywhere

 Morgan James makes all of our titles available
through the Library for All Charity Organizations.

www.LibraryForAll.org

CPSIA information can be obtained
at www.ICGtesting.com
Printed in the USA
LVOW07s0028200917

549348LV00002B/386/P